W9-DES-808

WHAT CASINOS DON'T WANT YOU TO KNOW

JOHN GOLLEHON

CARDOZA PUBLISHING

GAMBLER'S BOOK CLUB

Get all your gambling books at Gambler's Book Club (GBC) in Las Vegas, and enjoy the world's largest selection of gambling and gaming books—more than 3,000 titles in stock!

702-382-7555
www.gamblersbookclub.com

Cardoza Books by John Gollehon
Conquering Casino Craps
Commando Craps & Blackjack!
Casino Games
What Casinos Don't Want You to Know
Attack the Casino's Vulnerable Games

To Skeezer...My Best Buddy

Your decision to gamble is a personal one. It should take into account many things, not the least of which is your ability to wisely manage money. If you frequently overdraw your checking account, exceed your credit-card limits, or otherwise spend your money recklessly—buying on impulse, for example—suffice to say gambling is a bad idea. If you do decide to try your luck, promise yourself that you will stay within your means. Playing craps can be fun. Don't let serious losses take your fun away.

Cardoza Publishing is the foremost gaming and gambling publisher in the world with a library of more than 200 up-to-date and easy-to-read books and strategies. These authoritative works are written by the top experts in their fields and with more than 10,000,000 books in print, represent the best-selling and most popular gaming books anywhere.

NEW REVISED EDITION!
Copyright © 1999, 2004, 2012 by John Gollehon
-All Rights Reserved-

Library of Congress Catalog Card No: 2011940302
ISBN 13: 978-1-5804-2303-8   ISBN 10: 1-5804-2303-5

Visit our website or write for a full list of Cardoza Publishing books

CARDOZA PUBLISHING
P.O. Box 98115, Las Vegas, NV 89193
Phone (800)577-WINS
email: cardozabooks@aol.com
www.cardozabooks.com

TABLE OF CONTENTS

INTRODUCTION

Casinos would much prefer that their customers have no plan, no strategy, no discipline and no skills. For the most part, casinos are getting what they want, with so many new players coming on board as new casinos are built. This new market of unsophisticated players has become a gravy train for the casino industry.

Can you imagine an army marching off to war without a plan, a strategy, without discipline or skills? Well, that's basically what casinos are faced with today. Don't we all wish we owned a casino somewhere, anywhere? If you don't want to be easy pickings anymore, at least you've picked up the right book!

I particularly appreciated receiving this letter from one of my readers: "John, just a note to tell you how much your books have helped me, particularly in the way I bet. I play with more confidence now. I'm no longer afraid to bet heavier when I'm winning. A friend walked up to me at a craps table last week and asked if the stack of black chips in front of me and the ones on the pass line were mine. Before I could even say yes, the number hit and I collected two $500 chips in the pile! John, I owe you one!"

Some of my tips in learning how to bet aggressively yet wisely apparently hit the target for this reader. The idea of increasing your bets in planned increments as you continue to win is what the letter-writer was alluding to. It means having a strategy and using it, as opposed to some haphazard scheme of gambling with no basis of merit. In this book, we'll talk about betting—when to bet big and when to bet small, how to determine when to lay off or go full steam, and which games give you the most bang for your buck. Sure, I've covered these topics in some of my other books, but this time I'll show you a way to bet that's even better and easier to accomplish.

Of course, before you decide to gamble, you should take into account many things, not the least of which is your ability to wisely manage money. If you frequently overdraw your checking account, exceed your credit card limits, or spend your money recklessly by buying on impulse, gambling is a bad idea. If you do decide to try your luck, promise yourself that you will stay within your means—and I'll help you by giving you some proven money management techniques that are simple to follow. Gambling can be fun, if you don't let serious losses rob you of your pleasure. I'll show you how to do that and more in the easy-to-read, no-nonsense chapters that follow.

I want to get you in the right frame of mind so that you can apply the skills I teach you in this book to defend yourself against the casino with the best arsenal of weapons available. I call it psychological warfare but unlike Rambo, you'll be carrying your weapons in your mind—the ultimate camouflage!

1

THE #1 SECRET OF WINNING: KNOWING WHEN TO STAY

In my earlier writings, I talked about the importance of being happy with a small win, and then seemingly contradicted myself by emphasizing the importance of not setting any limits on your winnings. At least that's what a lot of readers told me in their letters.

Well, it's not contradictory. Successful gamblers must appreciate a win—a pure win, any win—and at the same time, appreciate knowing that there is a chance for a big win, a win without limits, an anticipated win. Good gamblers will always set their sights high as they relish the anticipation that drives them to bigger wins. Without this drive, small wins may be all they can achieve. Possessing both qualities is fundamental to becoming a successful gambler.

It really isn't that complicated, but it isn't easy to explain either. So let's talk about a *pure* win first because it is by far the most important. Believe this: You can't win big if you don't know how to win small. Let me tell you a personal story that might clear things up. It was our first crack at the dice tables and the seas were choppy. My friend was doing everything he could to force wins with his betting. "Bobby, you're betting that hard 10 like you think you can force it out," I warned him. "The dice don't know how much you've got on that number."

"It'll hit!" he answered. It didn't. I already had my business meetings out of the way and we were at that point in the day we had looked so forward to, but things weren't going as planned. After a half-hour at this table—a half-hour that seemed like two hours—I counted my chips again to confirm that I was actually up a hundred bucks. Not enough to buy a new Benz, but it was a win and with the table as rough as it was, I was pleased that I had survived the casino's first salvo on my money. I walked. And you know what? Under the circumstances, I was very, very happy to cash $100!

After a short trip to the coffee shop, I meandered back to that table to see if I wanted to jump in again. My buddy was still there. He was on his third marker. We just looked at each other. There was no need for words. I walked away because I knew what was happening and I didn't want to witness it. My trip back to the table confirmed for me exactly why I had walked away the first time. You see, that $100 win turned out to be much more than a win—it was a win in place of a loss!

A gambler who knows how to appraise this type of situation may add it all up a lot differently than you might. You might say, "Well, he started with $100 and walked away with $200 so he won $100." That's the wrong way to size it up. I could have easily stayed a few more hands and lost the $100 in winnings and then lost my entire $100 stake. As it turned out, that's exactly what would have happened if I had stayed. If we add things up based on that scenario, we realize the difference in standing on $200 or more, depending on the limits I would have set on my losses and whatever limit I would have set—and I can assure you, that's the limit I would have hit.

Instead of being down $100 or more, I was up $100. The win prevented a loss. No matter how small, think of your wins as a win against a loss. If you won, you didn't lose. Wins prevent losses—and a gambler's first objective is to protect against losses! Too elementary for you? Well, it is elementary! And if you would rather not have taken your winnings, electing instead to fight on under adverse conditions, there's nothing left to explain, is there?

> A gambler's first objective is to protect himself against losses

Take the pure win and run like hell! I call it "setting your sights on the win." And when you do win, stop a minute and grasp those chips in your hands and thrust them into the air like you just won the Oscar. I want to teach you to regard your winnings, no matter how small, as a major accomplishment. I want you to be able to enjoy that incredible state of mind. I've always believed it's the mark of a truly outstanding gambler.

There's a line in Paul Newman's old movie, *Winning,* that I particularly like. When describing Newman's character, his girlfriend says, "He doesn't care what he's racing for or how much the purse is. He just wants to win!" It's difficult to balance a pure win and a big win (we'll talk about big wins in the next chapter), but that's the way it has to be. They must be delicately in balance. The secret is in knowing that on one scale sits a state of mind and on the other scale sits a state of opportunity. If you remove one from its scale, the other side falls.

I hope my story helps you understand what a pure win is all about. A pure win is not measured by how much. In fact, there is no measure at all. If you're one of those unfortunate souls who can only define winning by how much you won—if that's all it is to you—then I can't help you. The next time you play, you'll know if any of this has soaked in. The next time you throw a nickel chip on the hard eight and it hits, your reaction will tell the story. I only hope you don't stand there complaining because you didn't bet a dime!

QUITTING WINNERS

Let's return to my story for a moment. When I left the table, I quit winners. I walked away a winner, plain and simple. My friend didn't. As I recall, he was up a little at the time I left, but he elected to keep playing and proceeded to give back whatever winnings he had made to that point, and he continued to lose more and more. We both had the same feelings about the table. We were not the least bit positive about it. The right move was to leave, particularly since we had managed to actually win during a difficult session through judicious betting. Besides, my friend was becoming reckless in his betting—another sign that it was time to quit, take a break, and maybe try it again later. It was as if he had forgotten what a win really is.

A few dollars? A hundred dollars? Is that a win? Not to him apparently. Sometimes he's so screwed up he thinks losing a little is actually winning; he's happy if he only loses a few hundred. Needless to say, I don't see this guy anymore, let alone play with him. He's too depressing.

ALL OR NOTHING AT ALL?

There's yet another facet of this rather simple story that needs to be addressed. Many gamblers in the position I was in would have elected to make a different decision at the time I left. Many would have reasoned that the table was tough, a break-even would be considered good, so why not risk the $100 in winnings in heavier betting in the hope the table would turn when a new shooter came out! I see this tendency all the time. And the casinos love it.

Here's what those players are thinking: A few piddling chips are not worth the trip to the cashier's cage, so why not give it one last hurrah and see what happens. Bad thinking! What happens is exactly what you might guess. They almost always walk away with nothing to show for their effort. The same thinking applies when that $100 stake has dwindled to just a few piddling chips. You started with $100 and you're down to $20. You risk the $20 in one shot and you lose it. That $20 might have been good enough to start another session; it could have been your stake for the next go. But no, it's now in the casino's coffers, along with the rest of your money. The casino got it all!

When the table's not cooperating, when it's time to leave, take all the chips you have in front of you and head for the cashier's cage. Don't play them off. That's the mark of a loser. I firmly believe that the thing that separates winners from losers is much more than luck and even much more than skill. It's an uncanny ability to just know when—when to jump on it, when to ease back, and when to walk.

> Winners know when to jump on it, when to ease back, and when to walk.

PRESS ON!

I have a friend in Southern California who is one of the best racehorse handicappers I've ever met. He's young and he's a little reckless, but he can pick winners. The problem for him is leaving the track with his winnings. No, he doesn't get mugged; he simply mugs himself. He has the same tendency so many bettors have, experienced and inexperienced alike. He bets his winnings right back in the next race, and then the next, and goes home broke. This, dear reader, is not being aggressive. It's being stupid. Please don't confuse being aggressive with being stupid. Maybe the following story about my friend will not only help you understand the thin line that separates the two, but will also help you to avoid this crucial mistake.

David hit a few nice win bets in the early races at Santa Anita and parlayed most of it in a fifth-race exacta box. He picked three horses; he was sure two of those three would cross the line first and second. And he was right. He collected a whopping $583.00 at the window. But from there on, it was all downhill for three races. I never saw a bettor throw his money away so fast and so recklessly. It's what I call "trying to force the outcome by the way you bet." You can't force the horses. You can't bet your way into the winner's circle. A bigger bet is not going to increase your chances of winning. The only person at the track who can legitimately "force" the horse is, of course, the jockey. And as I recall, David was not wearing silks that day.

By the ninth race, he was ready to get it all back with another bet on the nose of a 6 to 1 claimer. He didn't. He went home virtually broke and there was absolutely no reason for it. He may be a good handicapper, but he's a poor bettor. And it all comes from the fact that he's lacking in discipline. Severely. I've never seen the inside of his house, but if I did, I'm sure there would be dirty socks lying around, dirty dishes in the sink, and a half-eaten pizza on top of a stack of racing forms. He's a good kid, and I really like him. But he takes a desire to win way beyond aggressive. He eats, sleeps and breathes racing. He has everything else going for him. He just has no concept of knowing *when*—when to be aggressive and when not to, when to bet and when to watch.

But an interesting thing happened to David this year. He caught some really huge trifectas at the track—and he went home with all the money! Believe it! No, it wasn't because he learned his lesson exactly. It's just that every one of his big hits came in the ninth race, the last race of the day. He had to go home with it—there were no more races! To all the Davids of the world, I hope all your ninth races are happy ones.

> You can't win big if you don't know how to win small.

PRACTICE WHAT YOU PREACH

I remember the time I went to a harness race with a friend and hit a $100 trifecta in the second race. When I got back to my table with two fifties, he said, "Stuff one of those fifties in your back pocket."

"Oh, I've got enough discipline to keep some of it," I answered. "I don't need to play that little stuff-it-in-your-pocket game. That's been part of the advice in my lectures ever since my first book." This guy was giving *me* a lecture!

The rest of the night was not so good. The track was sloppy and we might as well have thrown darts at the program. Picking these horses was purely a gamble. The minor tracks for harness racing are very difficult to handicap, regardless of the track conditions. But on we went, making little $2 bets that made us just a part of the crowd. We had fun but there was no real excitement for me since I had purposely filed away any plans of betting aggressively. This just wasn't the place, and certainly not the time to do that.

When I got home late that night after a long drive, I headed straight to the hamper to dump my clothes and then into the shower. But I kept thinking about how I came out for the evening. I always keep detailed records on each program, race by race—a balance sheet, if you will—so that I can see exactly how well I did or didn't do and try to learn from it. I staple all the losing tickets to the program and then save it, which I highly recommend if you're ever audited and plan to show losses at the track against reported winnings. I couldn't figure out why I came home with only a few dollars when I should have won about $75 according to my program records. I counted the money in my wallet again and then looked over the program again, thinking I must have added wrong.

And then it hit me! I rushed to the hamper, found my pants and rummaged through all the pockets. There it was. A nice, crisp, $50 bill! When my buddy told me to stuff it, I did, but I had forgotten about it. What a pleasant surprise! My friend had taught me the same lesson I've been teaching gamblers for nearly two decades. Now I practice what I preach. My back right pocket is for winnings—winnings to go home with.

2

THE #2 SECRET OF WINNING: KNOWING WHEN TO LEAVE

During a talk-radio interview several years ago, the host asked me a question that I thought was particularly trite: "Why do you play, Mr. Gollehon?" Before I started to answer him, I realized the host was trying to trick me. Had I answered, "I play to win," as he expected me to do, this guy would have really unloaded on me. Even a trite question doesn't deserve a trite answer. "Why do you play?" is a serious question. And the answer, for me at least, goes far beyond what the talk-show host could ever have imagined. Let's just say that during the remainder of the interview, the host and his audience got more than they bargained for.

Like that interview, this chapter will reveal more about your interest in gambling than you've ever realized, and it should help you a great deal in your future play. Where the first secret of winning dealt with a small win (and taking it home), this chapter leads to the other end of the win spectrum—the big win. It is at that end of the spectrum where the casino hopes you never venture. But if you do enter the realm of the really big win, the casino will smile (never showing their true emotions) and hope you don't go home with it. No doubt about it, the second secret of winning is the biggie—but remember, one doesn't work without the other. Okay, you've got the idea. Now let's get down to serious business.

I believe there are three basic reasons why people gamble, but only one is the real key to finding unlimited success. We should talk about all three reasons though, so we'll start with the first. It's so obvious that it couldn't possibly be the key. It goes without saying, but we have to say it anyhow: Gambling is fun! Without the element of fun, you probably wouldn't play. If playing blackjack or whatever your poison weren't fun, five will get you ten that you'd give it up. It doesn't take a Princeton Ph. D. to figure out that people like to do things that are fun, and don't like to do things that aren't. If you had a choice between digging a ditch and going to Vegas, my gut feeling says the ditch will have to wait.

But fun alone doesn't make it. Picture yourself playing blackjack with "play" money. You're playing but there's no anticipation of winning. Of course I mean winning with *real* money. Most psychologists will tell you that risk is the key factor; that without the risk, there's no excitement, no tingle. I've never totally subscribed to that theory, though unfortunately, there is good evidence to support the claim.

LET'S MAKE IT INTERESTING

We all know people who gamble just to make things interesting. They like to wager on just about anything. On one hand, it's an innocent trait, but on the other hand, it might be a telling sign of trouble. Clearly, it can lead to degeneration. In the casino, certain danger signs identify players on the precarious path: They have no plans or preparation because it isn't important to them. They offer no scrutiny of the tables or machines because it isn't important either. And you can bet they've left all their disciplines at home, if they had any to leave, because plain common sense would or should stop them before they hurt themselves. For these players, the number one thing to do when they first arrive is rush to the tables. They are in need of a fix—they want to quickly become at risk! This type of problem player is best exemplified by sports bettors who wager on a game just because it's on TV and they plan to watch it. These unfortunate souls can only be interested in the game if they are in action. They have reached the point of compulsion.

On the other side of this delicate line is the golfer who likes a friendly wager "to make things interesting." I know this well because I like to gamble when I play a round of golf, but my reasons are completely innocuous. I like golf because it is such a complex and keenly competitive sport. I take the game seriously. I don't want to go out with a six-pack and just hack around. I particularly like playing with friends who also play seriously, and also enjoy a friendly wager. With money on the line, that little three-foot putt seems to take more concentration, and it's not because of the risk of losing a few bucks. A few bucks are not enough to tingle me and besides, I've got enough tingles standing over those darn three-footers. I don't need any more tingle than that!

What's important here is that the wager has nothing to do with making the game interesting. The game is already interesting. For me, the wager has simply added another facet of competition beyond competing to better my own score and the score of my opponent. It's like we've created our own little tournament. Of course, there must be no aggression. I'm not out trying to gouge money from my friends. We all feel the same way. So if you find yourself gambling on typically non-gambling events, I urge you to recognize this important difference. I can enjoy a round of golf without wagering; I can enjoy watching a football game without wagering.

Can you?

THE CRYSTAL BALL

I believe there's something else that really drives successful gamblers. It goes far beyond fun, and has little to do with risk. It's what separates winners from losers, even big winners from average winners. It's that important. Some players have it; most don't. Read on and see if you can grasp the key. If you can, you're on your way to becoming the best player you can be.

Suppose you're getting ready for a trip to Las Vegas—not a vacation, mind you, but a gambling trip. Then someone calls and tells you that you're going to go out there and break even. That's right, someone with a crystal ball tells you exactly how the trip is going to turn out. Play along with me.

You're going to hit the tables for five hours on Friday night, another five hours on Saturday, and most of the day on Sunday. Maybe a few more hours on Monday morning before your plane leaves, and after all that, you're going to come home with exactly what you had when you left, less your expenses of course. Your trip will boil down to a lot of work, no rewards. All of a sudden, the fun aspect of your trip has disappeared and play takes on the appearance of work. Think about it. You're going to endure the long flight out there, screw around with the rental car company, argue with the hotel about your room (it has a nice view of the loading docks), play your ass off, stuff all your dirty clothes back in your suitcase (that's funny, everything fit when I packed it!) and scurry off to the airport to catch that long flight home. And all you will have to show for it is, well, a suitcase full of dirty laundry. No big winnings. Not even little winnings.

Would you still go?

Think about it. Would you go? No? Not Sure? If you're like me, you'd stay home, not so much because it wouldn't be fun anymore although that's important, but mostly because you would no longer have the anticipation of winning—especially, the anticipation of winning big. You already know how you're going to do. You're not going to win a damn penny!

Let's change the scenario a little. This time your friend with the crystal ball tells you you're going to go out there, play all those hours, and lose a grand. You're either going to come home short one big one or expecting a little envelope in the mail from the casino a few days later with a note inside that says, "We hope you enjoyed your stay. Your marker balance is $1,000.00. Please use the enclosed postage-paid envelope to remit your check." Hmm. Now do you want to go ahead with your plans? You've been waiting for this trip a long time and what the hell, you've lost more than that before. Besides, losing a thousand is about what you would have expected. Or feared.

So what do you think? Are you still going to go? Of course you're not! At least you shouldn't, unless you just don't care anymore.

Let me give you one last peek at the crystal ball. This time you know you're going to have some modest success at the tables and come home winning $1,000. Would you go this time? Most players probably would. But in my case, I'd stay home. It's not that I know I'm not going to have any fun, because I probably will. It's not that I know I'm not going to win, because I do know I'm going to win. The problem for me, and the reason I don't want to go, is that I know I'm *only* going to win $1,000. What's missing for me is not the fun element and it's not the winning element. It's the winning big element. Knowing that my winnings will be limited to $1,000 has taken away my anticipation of winning big.

Don't confuse this important factor with what we covered in the first chapter. If I did go to Vegas without the advantage of a crystal ball and scratched and gouged my way to a $1,000 profit, I would have been very happy with it. You know how I feel about that: I'm happy with any kind of a win. But during my play—up, down and sideways—I always would have been

thinking that I had the chance to catch a nice run and win big-time. It's why people buy lottery tickets. Why people buy racehorses. Why we all look at the stars and dream. That guy's crystal ball took our dreams away!

The dollar values in my examples are all relative. Maybe for you, a $1,000 win is what you dream of and is all the incentive you need to go. So plug in $200 for the second and third examples. Then look at it again. The point of my story should not be skewed by arbitrary values. What we are digging into here is the fulfillment of a fantasy. No one wants to believe that it's unattainable.

My examples were based on a pure gambling motive, not on a getaway vacation. That's different. The purpose of these theoretical trips was strictly to gamble. Clearly the express purpose of going out there is to win with the potential of really hitting the casino hard. You don't want to know how you're going to do, do you? All you want to know is that you have a chance of hitting the jackpot.

THE SKY'S THE LIMIT!

This belief of mine helps me understand something about lotteries that had always baffled me. Why was it, I wondered, that when our state lottery jackpot was at a mere one or two million, there was only an average number of players, but when the lottery jackpot grew to $10 million or more, people would stand in line for hours to buy tickets. Sales grew by leaps and bounds the higher the jackpot grew. When our lottery jackpot hit $25 million, getting tickets was like trying to buy tickets to the Super Bowl.

The $1 million jackpot was seen by people as a "limit." It was simply a minimum starting point from which the lottery would grow. But $10 million far exceeded this limit and offered the players what they viewed as being beyond their wildest dreams. It's hard to figure some people. It's even harder to figure the masses. Doesn't a measly $1 million fall into the realm of "beyond your wildest dreams?" It does mine. I don't want anything to limit my anticipation, but isn't a $1 million limit high enough? For some lottery players, apparently not. Of course, it's only worthy of discussion for the sake of making a point. I don't play the lottery and you shouldn't either.

Perhaps a better example can be found at the racetrack. Horseplayers are usually broken down into two distinctly different groups: those who play the favorites and those who like the longshots. When you play the favorites on what are called "straight" tickets (to win, place, or show), you are looking at short odds and limited returns on your bets. The only way that playing the favorites can have an impact on your financial condition is by making large bets (read, large risks). Yet this is the way many successful handicappers pay the bills.

On the other side of the coin are the players who like the longshots and the exotic bets. Exotics are bets that require picking a one-two or one-two-three finish, or even picking three or more winners in consecutive races. These bets present much higher odds against winning, but usually offer correspondingly higher payoffs. A winning $2 trifecta ticket (picking a one-two-three finish in exact order) with a longshot or two in the money can return 100, 200 or maybe 500 times your meager bet. Even the most disciplined handicappers are tempted and taunted by these silly bets, but the reasoning behind them is not silly. Clearly, the bettors who like to play exotics have a high anticipation of winning big. And I have great respect for that.

Once again the significance is the issue of limitations. When you make "win" bets, you know exactly what you are going to win if your horse crosses the wire first because the tote board displays the actual odds for your payoff. Not so with exotic bets. Even an educated guess is only a guess. All you have to do is watch the faces of those lucky bettors holding a winning trifecta ticket as they wait for their payoff to be displayed on the big board. First, the official sign has to be lighted and then the payoffs flash on the board. Win, place and show bets come first, so there is more waiting before the exacta and trifecta prices light up the board to the cheers of those holding a hot ticket. You can cut the anticipation with a knife.

Yet another example of how limits can be construed as taking away your anticipation of winning big deals with the original riverboats in Iowa. Iowa's legislature first set limits on how much a player could lose and how much a player could bet. To make a long story short, those riverboats ended up sailing down the river to Mississippi where there were no limits. The consensus of gaming experts was that the people of Iowa didn't want their legislature telling them how much to bet and how much to lose. But I believe the real reason it didn't work was because the people of Iowa didn't want their legislature taking their dreams away—the anticipation of winning big—by *limiting* their action.

If you don't carry this same belief, then we're not thinking alike and I probably can't help you in this very important aspect of gaming. The prime motivation for gambling should not be limited, and it certainly should not be limited to just having fun. Learn how to set limits on your losses, but never set limits on your winnings! If you follow me and subscribe to my belief, you can finish the next sentence: Why do I gamble? Because (all in unison now) I enjoy the anticipation of winning big!

THE KILLER INSTINCT

This drive only works for a certain type of individual. I'm not sure that you can simply learn it or acquire it. I firmly believe it has helped me immensely in my many years of gambling. A friend of mine calls it "a killer instinct." The anticipation we've been talking about can be translated—for me, at least—into a tremendously strong desire to win with the sky as the limit! It closely parallels what I touched upon at the very beginning of the book: I believe that what separates winners from losers is just knowing when. When to do what, you ask? In my friend's lingo, when to go for the jugular. A dice pit boss paid me the highest compliment a few years ago. What he said sums up this discussion quite nicely: "Mr. G., when a table's hot, we always look around to see who's there. We can only hope you're up in your room."

Indeed, a casino is no place for wimps. Remember where nice guys finish? But as I said, this hugely important trait might be an acquired taste or it might be an innate quality that simply needs to be developed. I really don't know, but what I do know is that the great majority of players, no matter the game, certainly are not aggressive. For them the anticipation is of just being there—enjoying the casino, the weather, the pool, the shows, and playing a little blackjack, video poker, or whatever.

You aren't aggressive enough if you don't feel it in your shoes like two Titan booster rockets—if you don't even think about the chance encounter with $500 chips piling up in front of you. And if you do think about it, you probably think only of its remoteness. If weather, a pool, palm trees and mountains (read: relaxation) comprise my anticipation, my reason for packing my bags, Las Vegas is the wrong destination for me.

Can you go after the big win with a businesslike tack, fighting hard in the trenches, yet enjoying yourself along the way? A friend of mine can. In fact, he claims that actually playing at the tables is one of his favorite forms of relaxation. Learn how to enjoy the fun of playing and the satisfaction of a pure win, all the while soaked in the anticipation of a win beyond all limits. That's the ultimate state of mind all gamblers should seek.

> Set limits on your losses, but never on your winnings!

3

THE #3 SECRET OF WINNING:

HIT AND RUN!

It should come as no surprise that the traits to accomplish what we learned in the first two chapters are individually classic. There are many conservative players who are capable of being tickled pink with a token win. And there is an equally large number of players who are capable of going for the big win—and I mean $100 chips flying everywhere—without fear or trepidation. The trick is marrying these two important facets into one psychological profile.

Picture in your mind the stereotypical "little old lady" who just hit the nickel slot machine for a whopping $50 jackpot. Do you expect to see her take that fifty and head for the nearest dice table with a look of determination that movie tough guy Bruce Willis would envy? I don't think so. But it isn't hard to envision her moving up to quarter machines, is it? Maybe dollar machines next. For her, this is the right kind of aggressiveness with which she can feel comfortable. She's simply staying within her element.

I can't overemphasize the importance of being aggressive—at the appropriate time—and setting your sights high with nothing but the sky as your limit. Perhaps the best way to gather in this trait is to look at it analytically. If we could look inside aggression, we would see two different pathways. One leads to generally good things while the other leads to trouble. Clearly, the wrong kind of aggressiveness can blow you out of

the sky! We want the sky to be the limit for your wins, not the limit for your losses.

Yes, there are indeed two forms of aggressiveness: a good aggressiveness and a bad aggressiveness. Of all the top players I know, all exhibit good aggressiveness; none show signs of reckless or careless play. Good aggressiveness may be third on my list, but that's only because it's crowded at the top. My favorite analogy of these two kinds of aggressiveness is cholesterol, a rather hot topic today with so much concern about the foods we eat. Everyone wants to eat healthy. I suggest everyone should gamble healthy too. Cholesterol is broken down into two kinds: The good cholesterol is called HDL (high-density lipoproteins) and the bad kind is called LDL (low-density lipoproteins). I like to think of the bad kind as being a cheeseburger with fries, and the good kind as a plate full of Brussels sprouts and cauliflower with a few soybeans as a nice garnish. Yummy.

In life, a good aggressiveness could simply be defined as a strong desire to succeed. Good aggressiveness bears the earmarks of a solid work ethic: lots of patience and a willingness to take chances. Few things of real value are ever just handed over to us; we all have to work hard, take the time and take the risk. No one can argue that there's anything wrong with that.

The bad aggressiveness can best be described as the way one goes about succeeding: stepping on people, taking advantage of people, using people, and even crossing over the boundaries of ethics and laws. People with bad aggressiveness want it all at any cost, and they want it now.

In gambling, good aggressiveness is increasing your bets *while you're winning,* even if it means not taking all of a nice payoff. It's not being afraid to bet heavy when you're on an incredible climb. It's also knowing how to bail out before you crash. Bad aggressiveness means increasing your bets as you continue to lose. This bad trait can have the same repercussions as in life, except that the damage is done mostly to one's self—but not always. The aggressive win-at-any-cost tirade can lead to much more than monetary losses: It can lead to a loss of your own self-esteem. Without a doubt, it can lead to an addictive, destructive world.

Bad aggressiveness is like the horseplayer in Chapter 1 who had that uncanny ability to win and win again, and yet go home broke. And it's like the guy I remember at the Stardust many years ago. In an incident I'll never forget, he lost bet after bet and then he lost his head. He went for the dealer, the pit boss, the security guard—hey, Tyson vs. Holyfield wasn't that good!

What kind of aggressive behavior do you harbor when you enter a casino? If you have the wrong kind—be honest with yourself—then gambling is a bad idea for you. In fact, you would be better served to have no aggressiveness at all.

THE DICE TABLE FROM HELL

It was like watching an execution. My notes say it was the summer of 1991 at a trade show in Atlantic City, but I really don't need the notes to tell this story because the incident left a lasting impression on me. Sitting across the aisle in a casino's gourmet restaurant was a strange sort of guy whose appearance was a dichotomy of characteristics. He looked rich and he looked poor. He looked like an executive and he looked like a bum. It was a good guess that he had money, but he appeared beaten and strung out. He was obviously late for something because he was eating like he hadn't been fed in days, but I'm sure he hadn't missed many meals, to which his 300-pound frame would attest.

I saw the guy in the casino shortly thereafter, at his "appointment" with a dice table from hell. His play confirmed

my first impression that he was one of the casino's better customers. All of his chips were pink, white, and orange with maybe a few blacks, and he was throwing them around like penny candy. "Another marker," he summoned.

What? I didn't see anyone throw a seven.

The guy still has all those chips working and he wants another marker? Oh, I get it. This is Atlantic City. It takes a month of Sundays to get a marker and a month of Tuesdays to get the actual chips. In Vegas, two fingers gets you two grand, but in Atlantic City, better known as "Regulation City," the rules say that each player must sign two different forms, turn in a coupon from Burger King, and sing the second stanza to "Yankee Doodle Dandy" before they can actually get chips to play with. That must have been the reason why this big shooter was asking for another marker. He figured he was going to lose the ten grand he had scattered across the table, and I guess he just didn't want to wait for more chips. Now that's confidence!

"Seven out!" Good grief, the guy's out of chips. No, wait. He's reaching into his pocket. All right! More chips! Just enough to tide him over till the marker comes. By that time, my friends had joined me and I filled them in on this guy's action. We watched him for about five minutes and it was like watching someone die a slow death. Why didn't he move? Why didn't he quit? This guy was totally out of control. We couldn't bear to see any more so we walked around the casino while I attempted to explain everything in sight to my friends, none of whom had ever been to a casino before. Nothing I said registered. It went in one ear and out the other. All they could think about was that rather large man, constantly combing his fallen hair with his fingers, throwing away more money in five minutes than any one of them makes in a year.

At the end of the evening, on the way to the elevators, I passed by that same table and found that same idiot. I have no idea how many markers he had gone through, but by the way the table looked and the few players left (I don't have to tell you what a cold table looks like, do I?) it was clear that he had been beaten badly. Here's a guy who presses his losses and watches them lose. He has no concept of quitting; he only wants to play as fast and furiously as possible. When he gets back to his office, his secretary will pay off his markers out of his personal account as routinely as she gets his morning coffee.

I know this kind of player all too well. He is his own executioner. He is his own worst enemy. Only the casino loves him. He's one of its better customers. Wait a bleeping minute, you say. I don't play like that! What kind of a lesson is that for me to learn? I'm not going to do anything that foolish. Oh yeah? Maybe not at that high-rolling level, but I'm willing to bet that many of my readers can see at least a little reflection in that ugly mirror. They just don't want to admit it. Sometimes, seeing an extreme example of your own weakness can be quite convincing.

I wanted to show you bad aggressiveness in its worst form: an unguided urging to press on and on, trying to force the win by the size of the wager. I've said it time and time again: In the casino, you can't force an opportunity. You can only wait for it to happen. The trick is being there when it does. You need the staying power to wait it out. We'll talk about that important facet of gambling in a later chapter.

The guy in my story actually had staying power, if you think about it—his credit line. He was almost certain to catch a decent shoot, blasting through all those markers. But by then he would be too far behind to catch up. Not surprisingly, even a nice shoot wouldn't have stopped him. He's the type who's never satisfied. I'm willing to bet that the only time he quits is when he's hungry or when his limo is ready to take him home.

> You can't force an opportunity—you can only wait
> for it to happen.

COLLECTING CHIPS

Allow me to segue into one of my own addictions. No, it's not gambling; it's collecting. I collect almost anything: coins, stamps, lanterns, old bottles, marbles, you name it. Antique shows and flea markets are my kind of place. I can kill a whole day at an antique market and drive my wife nuts in the process. But of all the things I like to collect, what I like the best are the casinos' black chips! When I'm gambling, I'm still in a collecting mode. I want to collect black chips. There's nothing nicer than having your chip tray filled with black chips. Of course, you can't keep them. You don't want to take them home with you and you don't dare give them back to the casino. What you do is sell them back.

How convenient. You collect these things all day and right there in the same place are people who will buy them from you. In fact, you'll get a hundred bucks for every one you've collected. There's no haggling, no negotiating. A hundred bucks cash on the barrelhead. How many times have you collected something for years and then had trouble finding a buyer? Well, not in the casino. The people who run these places, nice people that they are, graciously provide buyers to purchase all those chips you've collected. Such a deal! The place to find these buyers is called the casino cage where the casino keeps all its money. It's where you go to cash in all your chips. I'm telling you this in case you've never been to one before.

"Cage? What cage? I thought I had to play until I lost all my chips!"

Yeah, right.

CHANGING COLOR

Here's how to make this little gem of advice—the fine art of collecting—work for you. All casinos color code their chips by denomination. One-dollar chips are usually white or blue, $5 chips are almost always red, $25 chips are generally green, $100 chips are black, and $500 chips are usually white, pink or purple. As you play in different casinos, be sure to learn their color codes. It will be important to you, as you'll soon see.

I remember telling a dice-playing friend of mine when he was about to get paid off on a nickel hardway six to give the dealer a red chip. He wondered why. "Because you'll get two greenies," I told him. "The bet pays $45, so give him another nickel and he'll give you two greens. Now you can start your collection of green chips. Plus, it cleans up your chip tray. Wouldn't you rather get two greens than one green and four reds?"

As another example, let's say you're a place bettor and you managed to work up your bet on the six and eight to $60. If either number hits, toss a red chip down on the table and the dealer will pay you three greenies. The bet pays $70. Do you want two greens and four reds, or do you want three greens? It also works with the five and nine with a $50 bet. In fact, it works for a whole lot of bets. Just think before the payoff how you can maximize the payoff in larger denomination chips, and do it. That's how you can build up your "collection."

Of course, the problem comes when the table cools off and you're faced with giving the greens (or whatever color you're collecting) back to the dealer for smaller denomination chips to play with. Don't do this! Here's yet another advantage of collecting: You'll know when to quit. You quit when you would otherwise have to change color. Now, if it just so happens that the table hasn't cooled off and you continue to win, collecting will force you to move up the casino's color spectrum. Simply

increase your bet level to the chip color you were collecting. But do this only when you have a significant number of collected chips in front of you, and the table continues to show profit for you. Even though my examples are all related to craps, the same procedure can be followed at any table game. Simply encourage the dealer to pay you off in higher denomination chips as you continue to win.

Increasing your bets as you ride a winning streak is good aggressiveness at its finest, but it's difficult for some players to master. Now you know a great way to ensure that it happens. The key is in changing color. This "collecting" tip, my favorite piece of advice, forces you to do either of two things: quit or move up to the next color. If the table has turned sour, you quit and you cash in your collection. If the table is still decent, you proceed to the next color level, which should be the color of most of the chips in front of you. Got it?

One last comment: If you do decide to move up and the next roll turns out to be less than spectacular, I suggest you stuff the remaining chips in your pocket and head to the cage. It's time to sell your collection!

CHIPS ARE *NOT* CASH!

This discussion of collecting chips brings to mind another very important aspect of gambling: recognizing that casino chips per se are not cash. They need to be converted to cash in order to have any value.

I followed a story several years ago about an old couple that would always take some chips home with them so they would have a starting stake for their next trip. After several months went by and they returned to the casino, they were shocked to find that the casino would not redeem the chips, over a thousand dollars' worth! It seems the casino had changed its chips during the interim and had announced a cutoff date until which the casino would honor the chips (casinos call chips "checks," so if you're talking about chips and they're calling them checks, it's the same thing). Well, the nice old couple didn't care whether they're called chips or checks. They called their lawyer. I understand that a settlement was reached, but who wants to go through all that aggravation?

Cash your chips before you leave for home. In fact, cash your chips immediately after a playing session. Here's why: Let's say you had a big score and you're not well-known at that particular casino. Chances are the people at the cage will ask you where you got the chips before they pay you. You can yell and scream all you want to, and I can't blame you, but you'll most likely have to tell them exactly at which table and exactly when you won the chips.

The casino has two excuses for this procedure: First and foremost, they want to be sure the chips are not hot. They claim that stolen chips, especially in the larger denominations, are often turned in for payment. Second, there's the matter of Regulation 6A, which is intended to protect against money laundering. Generally speaking, you would have to present $10,000 or more in chips to be subject to this intrusive law, but casinos are keeping records of smaller yet substantial wins these days, because the regulation sets a reporting period of 24 hours to reach the threshold for these cash transactions.

I doubt the casino will hassle you over a stack of green chips for either reason, but they probably will over a stack of purple. If they know you, that's different. If they don't, be prepared to tell them where and when you won the chips. Someone will make a call to the pit and confirm that the table had a particularly large payout and yes, they remember you and yes, you'll get your money. If you can't tell them exactly where and when you won the chips, or if the casino can't verify your story,

you may be in for a surprise. Don't get the idea that chips are as good as cash. They're not.

Most high rollers know what to do when they have large denomination chips to cash in. They cash in the chips immediately and put the cash in a safety deposit box that the cage offers to everyone. Don't put the chips in the box. Cash them in first and put the cash in the box for all the reasons we just went through. A later chapter deals with all the reasons why you want to keep large amounts of cash in a box at the cage. It should be obvious but we'll cover it anyway. I see players every day walking around a casino or sitting in the coffee shop proudly counting their roll of $100 bills. They might as well hang a sign around their necks that says: I've got lots of cash on me. Do yourself a favor: Be discreet with your money.

HIT AND RUN!

I love this term *hit and run*. It's another mark of a player with good aggressiveness. And it means exactly what you think: You hit and you run. You win and you run. You win and you leave with your winnings. Quick and painless.

To make this important point today, I'm reminded of a Wall Street player who knows exactly how to hit and run. The analogy to casino gambling should be obvious. He lives in Connecticut and sees Wall Street once a year at best—yet he's one of its biggest players. His office in his home looks like any other office: fax machine, copier, computer terminal, speakerphone, and a desk that· wouldn't fit through most doorways.

What amazes me, though, is what he does in his office. In his own words: "I spend 90 percent of my time reading and studying. I don't invest in mutual funds because I don't want someone else doing my reading and studying for me. When I jump in, I know exactly why and exactly for how long."

What he's saying is that he doesn't actually "play" that much, but when he does, he's all business. He doesn't hang around. He gets in, he gets out. He minimizes his exposure. My old friend is the consummate hit-and-run artist. When I talk to him, I ask him what stocks he's got. That's an intrusive question but unlike the racetrack handicapper, he doesn't have to worry about the odds going down if I bet his horse. The more interest in a stock, the higher the price. Nine times out of ten his answer is, "I don't have any right now. I'm out of the market."

"Out of the market? What do you mean? Did you quit? For good?"

"No, no. Just for a while."

"What ever happened to your IGT stock?"

"I sold it last month."

"*All* of it?"

"Yeah. It split. I made a nice profit. I'm out."

"What's it at now?"

"Oh, it's still going up a little, but like I said, I made a nice little profit."

This guy not only knows when to get in and when to get out, he's not the least bit greedy about it. I remember his telling me, "It is the greed in people that keeps them in too long." And now I'm telling you, dear reader, if you can't learn from this wise old man's advice, you are a destined loser. How many times have you had a tray of those nice black chips in front of you—your winnings—and there's that little voice inside of you that keeps pushing you to keep playing. And don't you know exactly what will happen if you do? As sure as the sun sets in the west, you'll give those black chips back ten times faster than you won them.

You hit and you run—that's the bottom line. And about my Wall Street friend: He doesn't gamble.

4

THE #4 SECRET OF WINNING:
GRIND IT OUT

The term *grinding it out* can have different meanings depending on who's doing the grinding. Is the casino grinding *you* out, or are *you* grinding out a profit? Consider yourself a good player if you can hold your own while you watch other players come and go. As long as you can retain your original stake, hopefully grinding out a profit along the way, you increase your chances of catching that proverbial hot hand.

The casino's preference is to knock you out early. Less work, less headache. But you can go the distance if you exercise caution at the outset by playing it cool until you find opportunity. Indeed, the true mark of a tough player is using a conservative betting strategy to open play. That's what you do—don't argue with me. Then as play continues, your bets will depend on your successes or failures. If you falter, your losses will have been minimized. If you're catching a good hand, your bets will increase as your winnings increase. It really isn't that complicated.

One of the key advantages to this fourth winning secret is the ability to stretch out your stake. If you have a limited stake and the table's cold, large wagers will result in only one thing: a quick exit—without your stake! You'll have little or nothing left to start a new session. If you had started with minimum conservative bets to "test the table," you would at least be able to walk away with some ammo in your pockets.

You can't catch a hot hand if you're not playing, and if you're out of chips, you're not playing. Get it?

Let's review several of the games offered in the casino in terms of their staying power. Particular games work out better for me in explaining an important detail that relates to gambling in general. Let me stress that some of these games might not be the games you play, but read them anyhow. Otherwise you'll miss important messages that will apply to you and to all the other games.

CASINO CRAPS

Dice tables are a little difficult to compare to other table games because of the nature of the betting. Each decision of the dice doesn't necessarily win any particular bet or lose any bet. One bet might win while others are unaffected. Or in the worst case, all bets lose. It's a common fallacy to think that the more bets you are making, the better your chances of winning. Hot tables aside, what is more likely to happen if you make too many bets is your sudden realization that you're stranded too far from shore.

"Hey, I've got too much money out there!" You can do it with $10 on the line and $20 odds, another $10 on the come and $20 odds, a $12 place bet on 6 and 8—and before you know it, you're in deep water. The game just has a way of doing that to inexperienced players. The only time you want to increase the number of bets you're making is when the dice are passing and when you're ahead enough to justify the increase in risk.

The casino bosses like to see dice players make place bets. And it's not just because the percentages are higher. Place bettors have a tendency to make too many bets at once, thus taking away their short-term chances for success. The more bets you make in the short term, the greater the odds against you. Although the actual percentages remain the same, the odds of winning change by the number of bets you make and by the way you structure your bets. Here's an example: Let's say you make a place bet on the 6 for $12. If it hits, you press it to $24. If it hits again, you increase the bet to $30. At this stage, your original $12 bet has returned to your chip tray along with a profit of $12. The rest of $30 your profit remains on the table; and if the 6 hits again, your payoff will be $35. But it has to hit for the third time to actually do any better than making even money, assuming you don't take your bet down.

And that's another problem with place bets. It's almost customary to keep place bets up until they lose. Pass line bets and come bets are more like the typical blackjack wager where the player takes the bet and the winnings and then restructures the bet for the next hand.

THE FALLACY OF THE PRESS

PLACING THE 6 OR 8					
OUT	HITS	BET IS	BET BECOMES	TAKE	TOTAL TAKE
$12	FIRST	$12	$24	$2	$2
	SECOND	$24	$30	$22	$24
	THIRD	$30	$30	$35	$59
If the bet hits only twice and is not taken down, you have only earned even money on your original bet—$12 goes out, $24 is taken back.					

I'm using this betting system as an example because it's a common way place bettors press their bets, which is yet another problem with place bets—the tendency of most players to press them in the early going. This particular betting scheme—or any other betting scheme, for that matter—will have no effect on the place bet's percentage of 1.52 percent over the long term, but it will have a serious effect in the short term by increasing the odds against you.

If you have trouble understanding this, simply exaggerate the example. Let's say a bettor's procedure is to continually press the place bet on 6 until the player reaches the table maximum. On the way up this almost insurmountable climb, the player will get back only the excess of the 7 to 6 payoff odds ($1 per $6 wagered) as the player rides the 6 all the way to the top—a couple thousand dollars or whatever the table maximum is. As you can appreciate, the short-term chances of actually making money are virtually nil. Over a long enough term, however, the player will have reached the table maximum (how many times depends on how long the test term is), but the glaring reality is that by that time, the term will have become so long that the house percentage is almost certain to prove out. In other words, our theoretical player will have pressed winnings into losses.

UP A UNIT

In the preceding example, it is obvious that no players would be stupid enough to continually press their bets all the way to the table limits. But the example should help to show the difference between a player's odds of winning versus the house percentages. Clearly, players can raise the odds of winning— make them worse—by the way they bet, but they can never lower the percentages.

Full presses are not unusual at the dice tables, and pressing your bets when the table is hot can make you look like an astute player. But we all know that "hot" tables are not the rule; they are the rare exception. Accordingly, my betting advice applies to the norm; that is, the way a dice table plays in all but that rare occasion. But many players don't make their bets based on the norm. Greedy players bet as if the table's hot or about to get hot. Hot betting doesn't make for a hot table! A hot table gets hot when it "feels" like it. All a player can do is develop the staying power to be there when it happens—if it happens—and then take advantage of it.

This whole discussion should make it clear why I recommend making gentle increases in your wagers instead of full presses. One of my best playing friends uses the term "up a unit" quite often to increase his bets. If he's betting green chips, a unit on the place numbers 5 or 9 is $25; on the 6 or 8, the unit is $30. For the red-chip bettor, a unit is either $5 or in the case of the 6 or 8, $6 since the payoff is 7 to 6. Assuming the initial bet is $12 (two units), it would make a lot more sense to take the payoff on the first 6 rolled than to press it (pocket $14, give the dealer a dollar chip, and he'll give you three red chips). If you're so fortunate to see another 6 rolled, increase the bet to $18, pocketing $8.

You can also go up a unit with your pass line bets and come bets. Of course the player controls those bets; you don't have to tell the dealer what to do. And with the exception of the place bet on 6 or 8, the other place bets (and buy-bets on the 4 or 10) are really too high a percentage to make. So just think just pass line bets, come bets and place bets on 6 or 8. And remember to increase your bets by units: It's not only safer it's smarter.

THE STRING BETTOR

Years ago, casino bosses used the term "string bettor" to identify players who liked to place all the numbers. It was certainly an accurate term but I rarely hear it anymore. Most place bettors still "string out" their bets and cover all the numbers, usually right after a point has been established. It can vary from the minimal "$32 across" to "$12,800 across" including the point. When I say "$32 across," I mean covering all the point numbers—$5 each on the 4, 5, 9, and 10, and $6 each on the 6 and 8. And "$12,800 across" is covering all the point numbers for $2,000 each on the 4, 5, 9, and 10, and $2,400 each on the 6 and 8. This assumes all the bets are place bets, no buy bets on the 4 and 10. Before multiple odds bets were offered in the early 1980s, this was a common way for a high roller to get maximum action. But at great risk. Imagine the tension that had to be felt each time the dice tumbled down the table. A roll of a 7 would wipe out all the bets!

Whatever the bet, it leaves bettors standing on their toes. They need to see five or six numbers just to get their investment back. The way the casino bosses see it, one sweet 7 can wipe out all their bets—and that's the way you should look at it too.

String bettors put too much faith in the dice. They don't have a number that will win all their bets in one swoop. But the casino does. There is always that 1 in 6 likelihood of a 7 on every toss. S-W-O-O-P! It's like a pit boss told me years ago: "The players have a lot of things going for them, but we've got the 7!"

ALWAYS TAKE THE ODDS

There's another problem at the dice tables in terms of increasing your staying power: the odds bets, which is a "fair" bet in the casino. In fact, it's the only bet you can make in any casino, at any game, that doesn't have a house advantage riding on it. That's why it's important that you make this bet to the fullest. But some players begin a session with only single-odds in the mistaken notion that they are increasing their staying power. I've even seen players making no odds bets at all for the same ill-advised reason. You must always take the odds: Players who don't take double odds are clearly in the wrong.

But now casinos have upped the ante to attract customers by offering three times odds, and even ten times odds in some cases. You'll even hear about a casino from time to time that advertises 100 times odds on its marquee. Let's be reasonable here. We must stay within our limits for our betting. We don't want to get carried away with it all. It's nice that the casinos have offered us such a delightful treat, but if the dice aren't passing, the players aren't winning. The more they bet in such cases, the more they lose.

As a percentage difference to the player, the advantage of double odds over no odds at all is worth a little over 0.8 percent. But as the amount of odds you can take increases, the percentage differences become quite small. My advice has always been to take double odds at the least. If you can get three times or five times odds, do it. Any more than that could easily backfire if you get caught up in a losing game.

When I tell players they should back up their line bets with double odds, the answer I hear most often is that it would make their total bet too big. They don't mind betting $15 on the pass line, but they balk when they think about backing it up with $30. If the total wager of $45 is too large a bet for you, then reduce your pass line wager. Never bet more on the line than you can back up with at least double odds.

Of course, some players will argue back at me. Here's the most common response: "Yeah, but it really doesn't make any difference how much my odds bets are because in the long haul, they'll all average out to even." And that's basically true. In the long term, you should not win more nor lose less regardless of how many times odds you're taking. Here's my response to this dubious reasoning: Draw a line down the center of a piece of paper. On the left side of the line list all the bets you can make in the casino that will lose over the long term. You might be surprised to learn that nearly all the bets you could possibly imagine belong on the left side of the paper. They are all long-term losers! On the right side of the paper list all the bets that are even, no advantage to either player or house. The *only* bet that can be listed there is the odds bet at a craps table!

So I ask you, would you rather make bets that lose, or would you like the opportunity to make some bets that break even? That's the only choice you have. There is no third section to our piece of paper that lists all the bets you can make that win over the long term. There are none! Your two choices for the long term are real simple: losing bets or even bets. Which will it be?

Yes, I know it's a little different with sports bets, live poker, bets at the track, and even blackjack wagers. We'll get into that a little later, but for now understand that all bets made at non-skill-related games can only be divided into two columns, not three.

If you're a craps player, do yourself a favor. Take the odds and don't argue with me!

SPORTS BETTING

There are two commonly heard tips in this game of picking winners that I hear often. Both are alleged to have come from the top of the mountain on how to win at sports betting. Though they are pure fallacies, here are the tips:

Fallacy: If you want to win thousands of dollars betting sports, you have to bet thousands of dollars.

Fallacy: If you want to win thousands of dollars betting sports without risking thousands of dollars, you have to bet parlays and pick at least four out of four.

Both of these tips are not only worthless, they are costly. I pity the players who believe in such foolishness. In both cases, bettors would put whatever staying power they have in severe jeopardy. In the first case, since there is no qualification as to the bettor's financial standing, one cannot simply say that you must jump in with thousand-dollar bets. It's insane. And in the latter case, betting parlay cards—although tempting—almost assuredly will knock you out before the midpoint of the season. The flaws are easy to spot.

Let's look at these tips one at a time:

1. No one should ever make such large bets at the start of a season. Any idiot would know that risking thousands of dollars right out of the gate is more than a great way to win thousands of dollars—it's also a great way to *lose* thousands of dollars and all or most of your stake.

2. Never make large bets when your stake is static or dwindling. If your argument is that your stake is in the tens of thousands of dollars, you are not giving me a reason for betting a lot of money, you are giving me an excuse. Having a lot of money is *never* a reason to bet a lot of money.

By working a modest stake into significant profit through judicious handicapping, and betting only a modest percentage at any one time, a good sports bettor can reach the point of winning thousands of dollars through wise reinvestment of the winnings, not by risking the original stake. That's the way to do it! Some sports bettors will disagree with me on this point and suggest that the amount of money from which the percentage bet is made should include both the original stake, plus profit or minus loss. But I believe the original stake should never be jeopardized when a certain level of winnings is achieved. At that point, I base my percentage for the next bet only on my actual profits. However, if there are early losses and my original stake has shrunk accordingly, I make serious cuts in my betting percentage to increase my staying power. At a minimum, I want my original stake to last the season. Through judicious betting and handicapping, I've never had to face that problem.

By formalizing your bets as a percentage of your winnings—your "stand" at a particular time—it is clear that future bets will always be a larger amount if your stand has increased, and such future bets will always be a smaller amount if your stand has decreased. As is true with any form of gambling, your future bets should always reflect how you stand at that particular time. If you're up, you bet more; if you're down, you bet less. But risk your original stake only once. If it is ever out of risk, it should be put safely aside. Simple, isn't it?

BETTING PARLAYS

Now let's discuss parlays, one of my favorite examples of greed. I can't say that only greedy bettors are attracted to these things, but since so many are, one can assume that many sports bettors sport a little bit of greed. However, a more convincing reason why parlay cards get so much play is the increasingly large number of casino players in Nevada who now frequent a sports book. Betting sports is definitely on the *in* list in Nevada. Unfortunately, most of these inexperienced players don't know that parlay cards should be on the *out* list.

As we learned in the case of dice players who make too many bets at one time and thus increase the odds against them, parlays accomplish the same thing. But there's more bad stuff to go with it—parlays don't pay very well! In fact, some parlay cards pay worse than a keno ticket! Can you believe it?

Picking winners in four out of four games is a major accomplishment. In fact, the odds are (2 x 2 x 2 x 2 − 1) to 1. That's 15 to 1 odds. Guess what you're going to win if you miraculously pick four out of four? Try 11 to 1 on for size. The sports book has just shorted you four bucks in winnings out of every $16 you wagered. That's a 25 percent slap in the face! With parlay cards, you're bucking even bigger percentages, not to mention the incredible odds of picking a perfect card. I can't think of two better reasons to avoid playing these "sucker" cards. Show the sports book you're a smart player: Don't play them.

SLOT MACHINES

Most slot machines today feature credit meters. Coins don't dump into the tray when you win, they are simply posted on the credit meter. The problems with this clever little feature are twofold: For one, players tend to think of the credits in terms of points, not dollars. Let's say you started playing a quarter machine with a $20 buy-in. Now you're thinking about quitting and the credit meter says you have 80 credits. What you have is $20, not 80 credits. You're even! Hit the cash-out button and take your $20. Don't play it off as so many players do—that's the other problem with credit meters.

If you do play it off, you are effectively setting your loss limit at zero, which is the same as losing your stake. Remember our discussion about sports bettors who don't preserve their original stake? For many slot players, that's a given. Ask any casino slot department manager and you'll hear this response: "Most slot players play off their credits. We know that. We like that."

Indeed! Only the smart players cash out while they still have credits to take. That's staying power! Many players who play video poker assign a credit-meter loss limit of zero, risking both winnings and stake in pursuit of the royal flush jackpot. It's all or nothing for these players. As long as they have credits on the meter, they are in hot pursuit of the giant jackpot. There are only two reasons they quit: Either they hit it or the meter says "0."

The credit meter was a great invention for the casinos. Now that new technology allows players to establish credit on their slot club card and play from that credit, casinos are worried that it might be too easy to simply stop at some point with credit still available. The player would only have to pull the card out of the slot to quit. Any credit balance remains in the casino's computer. Credit meters made it too easy *not to* quit;

now, casinos fear that credit-card play might make it too easy *to* quit.

Another mistake slot players make is doing what they think is the right thing to do to increase their staying power. But it can backfire—and I'm sure you've seen this happen time and time again. Let's say a particular machine takes five quarters. If you hit a jackpot with five coins in, you win more than five times the win for a single quarter. Often the 5-coins-in jackpot is far more than the linear jackpot increases per coin, so what do you see players doing? They begin playing with only one or two coins in. They are plainly feeding a jackpot that they can't win! And imagine the hurt they feel when the jackpot hits, but only a few coins dribble into their account instead of the full payout.

Cutting back to one or two coins is not a valid way to increase your staying power. If betting five coins of a particular denomination is too high for you, drop down to a lesser denomination machine. The same is true for other machines that take three coins. Play the max: That's a good rule to remember. Similar to the problem of odds bets at the dice tables we talked about earlier in this chapter, some slot machines will take up to 100 or more coins per play. Anything more than five coins is bordering on the ridiculous. When I tell you to play the max, I'm only talking about machines that take three or five coins.

Whether you play on a credit meter, a slot-club credit card, a real credit card, or with real coins, play the maximum number of coins and try to quit when you're ahead. At the very least, quit while you still have something substantial left. What's left is the stake to start your next session. If you can do that, you have staying power. And win or lose, you can be proud of the way you play.

BLACKJACK

In a later chapter on betting strategies, you'll see that the best way to increase your staying power at the blackjack tables is to incorporate three strategies into your play:

1. Basic strategy for player options;
2. Card counting for detecting the ever-changing percentages; and
3. a betting strategy for protection.

In the days when I played only blackjack, one of the most common weaknesses I observed was a player's tendency to start out strong without any regard to the table conditions and without any regard to the deck construction. The betting strategy that you'll read about later in this book has many advantages to it, but perhaps the most important of all is *protection at the outset.* When I sat down at a blackjack table, I knew precisely what I was looking for—an opportunity. I also knew there was little I could do to force it out. I simply had to wait for it; I knew I couldn't simply bring it on by making big bets. Blackjack is a game of patience. If you have none, you have no staying power.

The only other things a player can do to increase staying power and thereby increase the chances of being at the table when the opportunity arrives is to play in a casino that offers the most player-friendly rules. Generally, these rules can all be measured in terms of *expected value,* and they all add up to one thing: a percentage. Knowing these values makes you a better shopper for the best rules.

Rule shopping is an absolute must for any seasoned blackjack player—and it's a continuous requirement because casinos like to change their rules from time to time. A new casino manager comes in and all of a sudden, you can't resplit aces anymore. A player gives the casino a beating at its single-deck table and all of a sudden there are only four-deck shoes to contend with. Hey, it happens all the time! If the change is beneficial to the player, it will be announced with fanfare. If the change is injurious to the player, you'll be finding out about it as soon as you sit down. "But I thought…" you say to the dealer. "Nope, we changed that, buddy," he flatly answers.

POKER

The key to poker is knowing at what point you can walk away from your investment. As you might imagine, good stock traders usually make good poker players. There are times to be conservative and there are times to be aggressive. But what you must do *at all times* is be sensible. You can't keep building up your investment if you have little chance of cashing it in.

Poker is the only casino game where the size of your bet—your exposure—increases as the game progresses. Similarly, the quality of your investment is also continually changing. If you want to be good at this game, you must know the basics of risk and reward. And where do you learn that? On the street! That's right, street smarts is probably something you're going to learn the hard way. But if you're going to play poker, you'd better learn it *before* you play.

Good poker players know how to stretch their stake. Staying power is key at the poker tables. They hold their stake precious to them, and they let go hard. But when they do let go, you can bet they're building up one solid investment. Poker is not the game for impatient players. Younger players tend to race through the games, hoping for good cards that rarely come. In many casino poker rooms today, the seasoned veterans clean up on the antsy newcomers.

If you want to play poker but you haven't yet played it because you're a little intimidated, here's what you do: First, bone up on the basics. You must know the rank of hands, of course, and the simple rules of the game you want to play. And they are simple. Next go to a poker room, pick a table with friendly faces and a tolerant dealer. Announce to the players and dealer that you are new to the game and might need a cue now and then. If the players are indeed friendly, they'll help you because they'll remember when they were new to the game. If the players are not friendly, they'll glare at you while licking their chops. That's your cue to move along to a more friendly table.

HORSE RACING WISDOM

"Hey, Bob, you want to go to the casino with me this afternoon?"

"No. All I've got is maybe fifty bucks in my pocket. I'd have to go to the bank and load up and I just don't want to do that."

"Okay. Then let's go to the track instead."

"Great! Pick me up in 20 minutes!"

Fifty bucks works just fine at the track, but it's not even close to what you think you need at the casino. You see, casinos want you to bring as much money as possible. They have you conditioned to believe that you always have less than you need to beat them. But if fifty bucks works at the track, why won't it work in the casino? It can! If you alter the way you generally gamble in a casino, it works just fine. What you must do is simply slow down, take a few breaks, and enjoy yourself. Resist the temptation to throw out bet after bet playing fast and furiously. There's no benefit to rushing through your bankroll. No benefit whatsoever.

At the track, all of this is taken care of for you. You can take several good shots at the exactas and trifectas with good earnings potential without exhausting your relatively small stake. And let's not call it small—fifty bucks is fifty bucks! For most horseplayers, fifty bucks gets them through the gate and all nine races! The racetrack is the easiest place to practice staying power. Go for it!

5

THE #5 SECRET OF WINNING:

DON'T PLAY FOR COMPS

Of all the things I see gamblers do or not do, there's one particular taboo that I find more troubling than any other. Comps! Most players today know what comps are: They are freebies the casino offers you, such as free rooms or free food, to encourage more play. The bigger your bets, the bigger your comps; the more you play, the more comps you get.

Pretty neat, huh?

Most players consider comps a good thing—something to work toward, something to win. But for most players, if not *all* players, comps are not a good thing at all.

In so many respects, comps remind me of "Tribbles," those innocent-looking, fluffy little creatures from a long-ago Star Trek episode. They were hard to resist: Crew members bought them by the armfuls, and eventually the entire Starship was overrun with them. (Am I dating myself?) But they came with a price. Well, the casinos' cuddly little creature-comps can become a nuisance too. They are one of the casino's most effective hooks that can snag your wallet right out of your pocket. I'm surprised how many otherwise well-disciplined players fall victim to the casino's most clever marketing scheme, thus playing right into the casino's hand.

Comps are not new. Casinos have been giving away the store since the days when casinos had sawdust on the floors.

Comps have a proven purpose—and that purpose is not for your benefit!

I don't play for comps. Why? Do I have to tell you? Because the casino wants me to do it! I don't do what the casino wants me to do because if the casino wants me to do it, it's not in my best interests. It's that simple. When I started doing radio talk shows on gambling, I quickly learned to avoid the subject of comps because I would always get into an argument with slot players who would call in and hog my airtime rattling off all the free stuff they got. It became a no-win situation for me, so I eventually learned to exclude slot club members from my assault on the comp scene. Hey, slot players are a tough bunch!

I am devoting this entire chapter to showing you the downside of playing for comps. It's a touchy subject, but at least I won't be interrupted by some maniac slot player. By the time you've finished this chapter, I hope you'll see that playing for comps is one of the most effective ways to either decrease your winnings or increase your losses—most likely the latter. Is avoiding comps a secret of winning? You bet it is! Read on.

$25 PER BET, FIVE HOURS PER DAY

The subheading you've just read is becoming a standard minimum among most casinos to earn table comps. And it's at the tables where most of the really big comps are earned, from first-class airfare to thousand-dollar suites and all the gourmet food you can gulp down. If you typically bet $25 per bet, five hours per day, I've got a news flash for you. Twenty-five dollars per bet, five hours per day spells disaster—like in Titanic!

Complementaries come with an assortment of pitfalls, not the least of which is the tendency to play only at the hotel or casino offering the comp. If you're working on a free-room comp at casino A, what's the point of playing at casino B? If things just aren't going your way at the casino where you're staying, you stay and play there anyhow. The casino's comp program is doing what it's supposed to do. You're not! There's also the tendency to play for more hours than you want to. Another hour at that cold blackjack table might get you steak and lobster for two, but how many people do you suppose you could have invited for that "free" dinner if you hadn't played that extra hour?

And then there's the tendency to bet more—much more—than you want to. The pit boss is watching you: You'd better get those green and black chips out there fast! You want to be sure your rating card looks good, right? But what about your wallet? What does that look like? Is it so fat you can't even get it into your pocket? Or is it so thin you can't even feel it's there?

Let me guess.

As you know by now, I like to make my point with a story or two. The point of the following story should become obvious. It's Saturday morning and I'm watching my friend play blackjack at Caesars. We both flew in on separate flights Friday night and were to meet with another friend the next morning at the tables. Not my first choice, as I would much rather have met in the coffee shop for breakfast. I finally spot him, and it turns out he's hungry too—I'm hungry for breakfast, he's hungry for blackjack!

I decided to just watch him play for a while, wait around for our other friend, and then go find a pot of coffee. As I watched him play, I couldn't help but wonder why he was betting so much, especially at the beginning of a session. Then I remembered the last time we played together and how he stayed at the tables much too long. Before that, my friend had acted like a typical recluse and usually would hit and run. Few bosses even knew who he was. But not anymore: Now,

he's friendly with bosses and casino hosts and he has become attracted to the notoriety he is receiving.

That's what playing for comps can do to you. And casinos know it. They take advantage of the need of most people to be "taken care of" and "respected." They take advantage of the challenge to "earn" as much from the casino as possible and, I suppose, to brag about it to one's friends.

Our other friend joined us as we finally walked away from the table. "I was at the Mirage last month," he told us, "and they gave me the biggest suite I've ever seen. I had my own chef to prepare my meals right in my suite! And you know what? I even had my own limo driver waiting whenever I needed him. Tickets to the fight? No problem. I got as many as I wanted. That's class, man."

WHAT DO ALL THOSE COMPS COST?

Any guess what all those comps cost? The cost is measured in losses at the tables. And for what we just heard, the cost is easily in the tens of thousands of dollars, though maybe not over one trip or two as he might actually have won once or twice. But you can bet your booty that when all his trips are accounted for, the casino is making out like a bandit. It's like a casino executive at the Mirage once said: "We give a good player maybe four or five thousand in comps. The player gives us $25,000 at the tables. Now, wouldn't you call that good business?" Indeed! Good business for the casino; bad business for the player. The casino is plainly showing you that it can be aggressive too. And it works.

But getting back to my friend at the blackjack table, he doesn't get the treatment that the other guy at the Mirage got, but it's close. They pick up his airfare, which is more than you might think it is: He flies first class, plus he always brings along a friend so that's another ticket for the casino to pick up. And he's comped at the hotel's gourmet restaurants; any show in town is his for the asking, ringside seats of course; he gets a limo, but he doesn't have his own personal driver; his suites are just average, not the thousand-dollar-a-day-chef-included variety. But what he gets or doesn't get is really not the issue. What's important here is how he got sucked into all this, especially someone like him. If it could happen to him, it could happen to anyone. Forewarned is forearmed.

How they got to him was through his ego. He heard too many of his own friends talking about all the great comps they got. Once he acquired the taste, he really enjoyed the pampering bit, and he knew what he had to do to earn it. He's not a good player anymore because he will always owe the casino. Every trip. He owes them for all the comps. He doesn't realize it, but that's the way he thinks.

Let me tell you how it works: For one, my friend no longer plays with his cunning hit-and-run approach. That would be too short; not enough time at the tables for a good rating to earn the comps. I'll let you listen in on our conversation as we left the blackjack tables en route to the coffee shop, but inadvertently rerouted to the nearest craps table:

"Come on Jack, let's take a break. The table looks choppy. Ham and eggs sounds good right now, doesn't it?"

"No, I can't. I've only played an hour here and I can't play tonight, so I'm going to finish the afternoon here."

"Yeah, 'finish' is the right word. By the end of the afternoon, *you're* going to be finished."

"Naw, I'm only betting a quarter on the line and I'm taking single odds."

"But even a quarter's too much here. And 'single odds?' What's gotten into you? You don't start with a quarter to be

safe. That's not safe and you don't cut down to single odds. That's stupid. Let's get out of here."

"Leave me alone, John."

What my friend is doing is more than playing for comps: He's purposely paying the casino back for those comps. He feels an obligation to return the favor, much as you do when you get a Christmas card from a friend who wasn't on your list. What do you do? You go out and buy a card for this forgotten friend. Psychologists have long recognized this trait of ours: We like to return a favor with a favor. Did I say psychologists? I meant politicians!

When you play for comps, you'll always end up owing the casino. You pay the casino back in your action—make that, losses—at the tables. Some players I know who play on comps and win big time actually go home feeling a little guilty, if you can believe it. Believe it!

Another way comps can destroy a player is by reducing—if not entirely removing—the adversarial relationship between player and casino. How can you be aggressive toward your friends? You must think of the casino as your *opponent*. The casino is interested in your money. You are interested in the casino's money. You can kid yourself all you want to, but the fact is that it's really not easy to aggressively seek out your friend's money. That's why I've always had a difficult time thinking of the casino as my friend. The casino is *not* my friend. The casino wants my money. The casino wants as much of it as it can get. Does that sound like a friend?

Can you imagine the Dallas Cowboys meeting the Washington Redskins at the 50-yard line before a game and exchanging high fives? There are friendships between some players no doubt, but for the most part these two teams just don't like each other. They are adversaries of the highest order. The team with the least aggressiveness usually loses. The team who wants the win the most usually gets it.

If you still don't believe me, let me tell you what a pit-boss friend of mine told me: "Mr. G., I have yet to stop a player and say, 'Hey fella, don't you think you've lost enough today? We don't want to see you lose all of your money.' Sure, we greet our good players with the highest courtesy. We make them feel at home. But our tactic is to get them in and get them out, minus their money of course. Hell, this casino pays for all the other departments. We don't make anything in the restaurants; even our hotel rooms lose money. We make our money right here in the casino."

So be a little leery when your friendly host puts his arm around you. Is he showing affection for you or affection for your money? When you leave, there will be another big player to take your place. He'll feel that same loving arm around him and see that same toothy smile staring him in the face. Some hosts I know are sincere in their relationships with big players, but you get the point don't you? Don't let a relationship, real or unreal, stand in the way of your goals.

Another reason to avoid comps is the almost subliminal way they tend to confuse your goals. Are you interested in winning comps or are you interested in winning money? Are you interested in winning big comps or are you interested in winning big money? And don't tell me you want both: You can't have both. You can't exercise the discipline to aggressively go after the casino with keen money management, smart betting and common sense, while at the same time trying to meet its comp criteria with undisciplined play. That just doesn't cut it.

The casino has very tactfully and very subtly changed your game plan without your even knowing it. They've changed your aggressive drive for winnings to an aggressive drive for free food, a free show, a free room. They've got you to the point where you chomp at the bit for what they want you to want. You've lost your number-one goal: to aggressively win money

from the casino without limit. Don't let the casino mess with your mind.

HIGH ROLLERS

We all know there are many rich players who wouldn't be caught dead betting red chips at the blackjack tables. Such bets would bore them out of their minds. And that's fine. I have trouble relating to that, as most all of us do, because I'm not in that league. But for those of you who are, ask yourself these questions: Am I playing only in this particular casino because I want to? Am I playing these long hours because I want to? Am I betting black and purple chips because I want to?

If the answers to all of those questions are "yes," then go ahead and fight for all the comps you can get. In fact, be aggressive about it. Negotiate. Tell your host, "I can do better across the street, so either give me your best suite or I'll walk." If you're going to be tough at the tables, you might as well be tough with your host too. And you don't have to worry about losing his affection: As long as you still have money, you'll still have his affection.

This discussion of high rollers playing for comps presents me with a double whammy: First, I don't like to see players beginning a session with large bets. It makes no sense. The high rollers' excuse, of course, is that they have lots of money and they need to bet at those levels to really enjoy gambling. Well, you already know how I feel about the excuse that having a lot of money is a reason for betting a lot of money, and that needing to make those big bets to enjoy gambling is equally inexcusable. Inherently, gambling is not fun, because the majority component of gambling is losing. Is losing fun? Not for me it isn't. Winning is the fun part. High-rolling gamblers must learn to appreciate the importance of timing.

> Good gambling is good timing.

So here are the high rollers throwing out big bets without any care or consideration of the table conditions. As I said, they have no concept of timing and they are playing "under the influence" of comps. Boy, that's a double whammy in the pocketbook if I ever saw one! High rollers prefer playing on credit. They don't want to carry large sums of cash with them on their way to the casino. That's a valid point. It justifies playing on credit, although it doesn't necessarily justify playing for big comps. At the tables, you generally need a credit line (or cash deposited in the cage) before you can be considered for big comps. Having credit in a casino can be yet a third whammy of high-rolling gamblers. Credit in a casino is a loaded gun pointed right at you. I urge you not to take the risk. Too many credit players set their line too high, and in casino speak, they "play to it." They play it away.

All I want you to know is that playing for comps, playing on credit, and playing aggressively for yourself is a tough juggling act. Only a few players I know have the discipline to set up a credit line and accept comps without shooting themselves in the foot. I love to hear that a high roller beat the stuffing out of a casino for tens of thousands of dollars and took all the sweet comps too. That's extra sweet. Just don't put more balls in the air than you can handle.

HIGH-ROLLER WANNABES

Most credit players fall in the $2,000 to $5,000 range, perhaps the most risky of all when playing for comps. Why? Because these players are in a gray area that's higher than a no-comp rating but significantly lower than a suite-and-airfare rating. Such table players who begin play with a bet that's higher than I recommend (you know, a green chip instead of a red chip) are most likely playing for a room comp (maybe only a casino rate on a room, which is half the usual room rate in some hotels). A room comp is about all a green chip is going to get you. If you're a $25 bettor and you want a limo ride to the airport, the casino is going to call you a cab. That green chip might get you a food comp in the coffee shop, but it won't even come close to getting you a gourmet meal. Hey, you get what you pay for. When I mentioned that most comped players fall into this gray area, you should know that most casino executives today see comping table players as a black and white issue. Technically, there is no real middle ground established by the casino; it has been established by the players, particularly those medium rollers who have begged their way up.

The modern approach casinos use to define comped players is simple: A player is either a good source of revenue for the casino or he is not. To help find the spot to draw the line between the two, casinos have created a new department called Player Development, which is made up of people who have the uncanny ability to talk out of both sides of their mouth. And you thought only lawyers could do that! They'll talk nice to a high roller on line 1, and talk down to a low roller on line 2. The guy on line 1 gets this greeting: "Mr. K! How nice to hear from you again. How's your lovely wife? When will I have the pleasure of seeing you again?" The poor Joe on line 2 gets this: "Forget it, pal, we're oversold this weekend. I couldn't get you a bed in the boiler room. If you wanna stay here, you'll have to pick a different time."

The marketing gurus in Player Development have created their own little chaste system. You're in or you're out, based on your wealth. The line divides the haves from the have-nots. But it's not your wealth per se that puts you over the line. It's your credit line that counts. Still, even that isn't enough to ensure a nice greeting when you talk to your host. You see, there's a glut of players out there with low five-figure credit lines who don't even come close to using it. In the lingo of the casino hosts, these players don't play to their line. Having the big line and not playing to it means it's just a status symbol for high-rolling wannabes, like a fake Rolex or a platinum credit card. Don't get the idea that you can set up a big line of credit, munch down all that great gourmet food, play timidly, and then expect a nice invite back. Forget it, pal! The casino will just write you off as a Great Pretender.

SLOT CLUBS

I mentioned at the opening of this chapter that some comps are arguably okay. That doesn't mean I like them or recommend them. I don't. But I know you, and I know how easy it is to give in and accept what seems like free stuff. I mean, who can turn down free stuff!

But is it free?

The most tempting of all are the slot club rewards. Slot clubs have become so popular that casinos are out bashing each other over the head to offer you a better deal. It's a players' market. So if you're a slot player and right under your picture in your high school yearbook it said you were the most disciplined student in class, then okay, let the comps come—but only without any special attention on your part, without changing a thing in the way you intend to play, and without doing anything differently.

For example, don't be tempted to play a dollar machine to earn more comps when a quarter machine is more your speed. Don't take a bigger bankroll than you normally would, and above all, don't play longer than you had planned. In essence, don't let the slot-club card influence the way you play. Some casinos will give you cash awards for points you accumulate through your play. Others will give you free buffets and even

free rooms. As long as you're not changing your playing habits, go ahead and take all the slot comps you can get.

But here's another twist on all this that I want you to read: The thought of earning all kinds of neat things just by playing the slots, something you intended to do anyway, sounds pretty good. It's like a bonus, a reward, a trophy or a plaque to hang on the wall. Some players think of comps as a mark of their accomplishment. Watching people stand in long lines waiting to sign up for a slot-club card as if they're entering a tournament would seem to be all the proof you need that you belong in that long line too. Come on, Mom, everyone else is doing it!

Let's look at it in still another way. Casinos located near metropolitan areas often run buses to bring the players in. The enticements are hard to resist: everything from free food to free money. Real money. The casino wants you! And they'll pay you to get you! To better understand the slot-club mentality let's compare casinos to airlines. Casinos offer slot-club points; airlines offer frequent flier miles. But there's a huge difference: No one purposely flies a longer route just to earn more miles. But you'd be surprised how many slot players are willing to go out of their way—translated, take more risk—just to earn more points.

I know too many slot players who spend more time checking their point totals than they do the machines they play. The rule is simple: Take only those comps that you would have earned anyhow, playing the same way you would have played if no comps had been offered. Whether you are a table-game player or a slot player, my hard-line advice to you is to forget about comps completely. I do. Today I play in complete anonymity, something you can't do if you're on record with a casino for a credit line or slot-club membership. We'll talk more about this important aspect of gambling in the next chapter.

A BRUISED EGO

With the possible exceptions I've noted, I hope you can see how silly it is to play for comps, particularly table comps, and how they can have such a negative effect on your play. I've seen horrible examples of how comps play on a person's ego far beyond the stories I've just related to you. Can you imagine a player begging a pit boss for a food comp after an hour's play? Here's how it goes: "Hey, I just came over here to see a friend. I mean, I played an hour and I would have gotten a meal easy back at my hotel, so what's the problem?"

"Sorry, sir, but your average bet was only $15 and that doesn't qualify you for anything."

"Aw, come on. Look, you're embarrassing me. All I want is a comp in the coffee shop for my friend and me."

"Your friend? No way, buddy. You'll have to excuse me now."

I can't think of any way to humiliate yourself more than to beg from a casino, yet players do it every day. And occasionally the casino throws them a bone. Take my advice: Leave your ego at home!

6

THE #6 SECRET OF WINNING:
MINIMIZE YOUR EXPOSURE

Do you often wonder if other players are doing better than you are? It's the way casinos want you to think. If it so happens that you lose often, it's human nature to think that you are forever cast among the losers, the unheralded minority, the unfortunate few who just can't win for losing. Fact is, the great majority of players lose in the short term, from session to session, from trip to trip. And all but the fortunate few are destined losers over the long term, over years and years of playing. With all those losing sessions piling up, a fourth-quarter comeback is all but impossible. Considering all the players I've watched over the years—and I've seen it all—I know there will always be a great majority of losers. There are losers who want to lose, there are losers who want to win, and there are—I swear—winners who want to lose, but there are very few winners who want to win.

I've been fortunate over the years because I play with a discipline uncommon to most players. If you were to play with me, you probably would be disappointed. In fact, you probably would lose track of me because I'm constantly on the move. I'm rarely at the same table for more than a few minutes and rarely at the same casino for more than an hour or so. I'm looking for opportunities. I don't expect them to come to me; I believe that I have to seek them out myself. If a casino is so busy that I can't "table hop," as the pit bosses call it, then I won't play there under those conditions. That's why I rarely if ever play on a weekend. If it so happens the casino is always busy, typical of a one- or two-casino market, you won't find me in that market at all. I need options. I need choices and I won't play without them.

On top of all that, I take a lot of breaks. You might have a better chance finding me in the casino's coffee shop or out walking. I need that break to clear my head, review my play, and make new plans. You don't see a boxer going twelve straight rounds without a break, do you? I'm amazed at how many gamblers play straight through for hours and then wonder why they got their lights punched out.

There's another important aspect of my play that you probably already know: I don't play for comps because I don't want the casino controlling the way I play. Besides, I don't play long enough at any one table to get rated. I move around so often that the paperwork just to keep track of my play, not to mention the hassle of showing a player's card to each new floor person, would be unproductive to both of us. But more important, my initial bets are not large enough to earn a comp anyhow. The last thing I want to do is try to impress a floor person. My preference is that they don't even know who I am.

When someone asks me how much I bet, I tell them that I always begin a playing session at the table-minimum level. That response usually draws a blank stare. And when someone asks me how long I play, I have another stock answer: "Not very long." It's a bit of a cocky answer but it says a lot. The last thing I want to do is let the casino's edge beat me down.

For me, it's real simple: When I'm winning, I play. When I'm losing, I don't. And the last thing I'm going to do is rush to play.

THE CASINO STROLL

One of the most important secrets of winning—last on the list but certainly not last in importance—is minimizing exposure. This attribute of winning was much easier to preach years ago than it is today. For some reason, the ranks of newcomers, mostly young players, want to do the exact opposite. They don't minimize their play, they maximize it! No patience, no breaks from the action. No time to develop a skill or a plan. A casino's theme song today should be "Fools Rush In."

One of the best ways to minimize exposure while enjoying the gaming environment is to simply wander the casino. But just don't walk with your head dangling unless you're looking for chips on the floor. Look at the tables. Look at the dealers, the players, the action. Are the dealers beating the players? Can you spot a table that looks promising? Why not wander into the coffee shop as I frequently do? Ah, so many places to wander! Let's do it together as I tell you about a couple of friends of mine who were not into wandering. See if any of the following sounds familiar.

DETOURS AND DIVERSIONS

I was in Vegas at the same time some of my friends were in town but I was staying at a different hotel. We had all played a day or so but not together, and had talked on the phone about how we were doing. I had the feeling that my friends were basically "played out" because their phone conversations were depressing. So I suggested meeting at the Desert Inn, one of my old haunts of years ago, and then walking over to Treasure Island to watch the pirate ships battle—not particularly exciting, but I had my reasons.

Next I had planned to walk them back to the hotel and show them the Desert Inn's golf course, maybe even hit a few balls on the driving range. On our way back to the casino, I planned to walk them by one of the eleven hot tubs scattered around the property, the one I had always considered my own personal tub. The landscape around that section of the grounds was pure tranquility. Then I wanted to stop by the pool, find some chairs, and just basically enjoy the weather. It was one of those October days in Vegas—the best time to visit—when being outside just seemed to make more sense than being in a stuffy casino.

You can see what I was planning, can't you? I wanted to get them back to the tables nice and slowly. Indeed my plan was to keep my friends away from the tables for as long as possible. They needed a respite from the bitter cold inside the casino. They had simply played too long and too recklessly, and I could tell they were determined to get even. I couldn't think of anything more dangerous to my friends, except maybe getting conked on the head by a golf ball.

To make this story short and sweet (or should I say sour?), we never saw the pirate ships battle; in fact, we never saw Treasure Island. And we didn't see the golf course either. Or the hot tubs. Or the swimming pool. They put their car in valet parking, met me at the front door, and made a beeline for the dice tables. You couldn't have drawn a straighter line from the front door to the nearest table. I didn't play, I just watched. Need I tell you how they did? Like I said, they were determined to get even.

I used this short story to emphasize my point about how easy it is to lose when you play with the wrong kind of determination. There's a big difference between being determined to get even and being determined to win—a huge difference.

But let's be clear on something: For players who tackle the undefeatable percentage games like craps, the difference will probably show up only in the loss column, particularly over the long term. A better discipline might result in smaller losses, not necessarily bigger wins. A conservative hit-and-run player might be able to restrict losses, but not necessarily increase the number of wins. These are the cold, hard facts of games where a negative expectancy rides on every outcome. You cannot "discipline" away the percentages. You can't hit and run your way to riches—not over the long term.

But there are games where the percentages can be beaten, where percentages vary, or where skill can overcome a negative edge. We'll talk about that in a later chapter. You probably think you're one step ahead of me, but I'm willing to bet you can't name the games. No matter. We're not ready for dessert yet anyhow.

SHORT AND SWEET

There is a positive aspect of all the games that we can talk about now. It's the aspect of short-term play where even games with a mathematical edge against you can be beaten soundly, if not consistently. I've always looked at my own play in terms of the short session. I keep my sessions short on purpose, and now you know why.

I told you about my Wall Street friend in the chapter on good aggressiveness to show you how he could summon his aggressive nature at just the right time, and then retreat with his winnings. That story could also fit into this chapter because he also is a great example of playing the short term and not "staying in too long." He knows what can happen, even in the stock market, in spite of everything you've heard about staying in for the long term. He takes his profits and he gets out. If only gamblers could do that too!

Short-term play can result in all kinds of wonderful and all kinds of lousy results. In fact, most gaming experts believe that you can throw out the small percentages in short-term play and I tend to agree with that. In the short term—a few hours, maybe a few days, maybe even a few trips—your bottom line will fall somewhere between "up a mile" to "down a mile." As the experts say, you can just about throw the percentages out the window. But why can there always be too much of a good thing? As you might guess, frequent short-term play can only lead to long-term exposure, each session adding up to the point where you've dug yourself a hole so deep you couldn't possibly see the light of day.

A nice little detour every now and then can help shorten the long term. A little detour can help clear your mind, freshen your attitude, and charge your batteries. We all need a detour every now and then, a break in the action. No matter which casino you're headed to, promise me you're not going to head straight for the tables. That's not what I call good aggressiveness and it's not determination either. Such actions are plainly obsessive. If you have an obsession problem, a good dose of cure could very well be one of the two "D"s I take when I'm gambling: Take a detour or take a diversion.

TABLE 1501

Regardless of where I stay, I always have a favorite table in the hotel's coffee shop, a table that I frequent regularly. I have several requirements for such a table: first, it has to be a booth; second, it has to give me privacy; and most important of all, I want to be sure the table isn't covered in green felt. I ask the hostess to keep the table open as often as possible (I hate to see someone sitting at *my* table). For this favor, tips in the $5 to $10 range are the order of business, but it's worth it.

My table at the Las Vegas Hilton is 1501, the first table in the "15" section of the hotel's coffee shop. It's right beside a much larger table that's reserved for the hotel's highest roller. Nobody else, and I do mean nobody, sits at that table when he's in town. For my table, I have to tip; for his table, the high roller gets a "reserved" sign. He also gets his own telephone and his own staff to wait on him.

"Water? You want more water, sir?"

"Yeah, more water. And bring me a couple more shrimp cocktails."

Meanwhile back at my table, I'm scribbling notes while eating a shrimp cocktail that cost me $9.95. And I don't mind paying for it. I'd rather pay for it than play for it. Right? But getting back to the matter at hand, I think of my table as a base of operations and more important, a place to go when I need a break. Table 1501 is my "diversion" from the casino. During my breaks, I think about the past sessions. What did I do right? What did I do wrong? Do I want to go to a different casino? Do I want to quit for the night? I don't like to make my decisions at the gaming tables. I want to get away from the tables to analyze all the factors without being influenced by the table's natural calling.

If you program your next trip with these simple detours and diversions, I can assure you a more controlled trip and hopefully, a more rewarding one.

ANONYMITY

We talked about it in the previous chapter on comps. I said that it's hard to maintain your privacy if you are signed up for slot cards and credit lines at the table games. Let's rack it up as yet another reason for not playing the comp scene. I can't think of a better place to have anonymity than in a casino, but anonymity also has another important value: It can help keep you in the short term.

Although my advice that follows might come off as being a bit arrogant, you'll see the importance of playing anonymously by yourself, or having complete control of your game plan when you're playing with others. To do this, however, you must be able to tune out the other players. And even if you're not a good player, the last thing you want to do is show off. Let me give you my worst-case example:

Many years ago, I had breakfast at the old Dunes Hotel with a writer who wrote for several publications on gambling. He was a good friend of mine who knew tons about gaming, but one thing he knew best of all: He didn't want to play.

"Come on, Phil, just a few minutes."

"Okay, but I'll just watch. I'd love to see you play."

On the way to the casino, Phil had to stop and make a phone call. I ventured on to the dice tables. A hundred has come and gone before Phil even got to the table.

"Hey, Phil! That was an expensive phone call!"

"How ya doing, John?"

"Fine."

Another hundred went down the slot and the chips moved one way: from player to dealer. Player to dealer. Player to dealer. I didn't win a single bet.

"John, is this how the game works?"

"Don't be funny, Phil."

"John, I've gotta run, but I'm glad I at least had a chance to see a real dice player in action."

"Go write your column, Phil."

I really thought long and hard about putting this story in my book. Despite the fact that it happened many years ago, it is still an embarrassment to print. But allow me to bare my soul to you because there are many good lessons in this brief encounter that might help you. For one, I know and I hope Phil knew, that I have no control over the dice's decisions at the table. I'm not a dice mechanic so I couldn't impress him with a string of 11's or hard 4's or whatever.

"Okay Phil, what do you want to see now?"

"Oh, let's see boxcars."

Like a short-order cook, I say, "One set of boxcars coming right up!" No, that isn't going to happen. I'm at the mercy of the gods of chance and I put myself in that spot. I set myself up. If Phil had said, "John, I understand you can hit a great seven iron," we would have gone over to the driving range and hit some balls. That would have worked. I hit a nasty seven—unfortunately, I hit a lot of nasty sevens on the dice table instead!

And one other thing: This little "exhibition" wouldn't have worked for a blackjack counter either. Phil only had time to watch in the short term, and even the best card counter in the world can't mystify anyone in just a few minutes. Play alone! If you have friends with you that think you're a good gambler, they'll be disappointed. They may even end up thinking you're a *bad* player. Ask any high roller how many times this has happened to him and you'll get story upon story:

"Hey, Louie, I hear you're a high roller."

"Uh, yeah."

"I want to watch you play."

"Yeah, sure, kid."

Fifteen minutes later:

"Hey, Louie, you just lost about five grand didn't you?"

"Uh, yeah."

"Wow! I'm impressed!"

Play alone. Otherwise, you might be tempted to "keep up" with your buddy: "You've got too much out there, Jerry. Whoa! It just hit. Nice job, Jer!" Meanwhile, you're looking at your lousy ten bucks on the line while Jerry's getting his stack of greens paid. So you think that if Jerry can bet that much—and that was a nice payoff—why not go to green chips too. Right? Result: "Seven-out, damn!"

My favorite story about letting others influence your betting comes from John Alcamo's *How To Avoid Casino Traps!*, in which he quoted a pit boss: "We once had five baccarat players from Brazil betting $50,000 a hand. Halfway through the shoe

one of our regular customers sat down to play. Two hands later, he left. He said his $500 bets made him feel cheap!"

Play alone—especially if you've written over a dozen books on gaming. You wouldn't believe the calls I get from people who want to meet me in Las Vegas and buy me dinner. The pitch always ends with: "And let's play a little blackjack together, too." The call that I can't forget came from some guy in Santa Fe. He opened with the same "I'll buy you a dinner" line. I told him, "Thanks, but I'm not really interested. I just got back, besides…"

He interrupts me with, "Then meet me there and show me how to win. I can make it worth your while."

"No. I really like to play alone."

So he says, "How about if I introduce you to my daughter. She's a knock-out!"

Unbelievably, these people think I'm going to show them how to win thousands of dollars in just an evening's worth of play. I'm not *that* good! No one is that good! My response is always something like, "Well, dinner sounds great, but I only play alone. And I'm not really comfortable trying to help someone win because there certainly aren't any guarantees. You know that, right?"

"Oh, well, forget it then." I don't hear a "Thanks anyhow" or even a "Have a nice day." Just a dial tone in my ear.

YOU ARE YOUR OWN TEAM

Most of the good players I know like to play alone. I know and they know that the game is between the player and the casino. I'm not part of a team—I'm my own team. It upsets me when I'm watching a friend trying to force wins by the way he bets. If I see my friend making stupid bets, I might be tempted to tell him so even though I know better. It's not unusual for my friends to ask me if the bet they're making is smart. And if I tell them it's not a good bet, they do it anyhow—and then give me one of those, "What the hell do you know?" looks.

Nothing good can come from team play. Losses tend to diminish in value when others in your group are also losing. If everyone else is losing, what's wrong with your losing too? It can make you think that way. And we've all had the experience of a friend standing beside us and talking our ears off. A blackjack table is no place for casual conversation. One guy wants to leave the table and go to another so he tries to talk the group into moving. Another guy wants to keep playing while you want to quit.

Your friend is betting too little during a hot streak and it bugs the heck out of you. You want to tell him to press up but you know better than to say anything. You also know that if you do break down and convince him to bet more, he'll get knocked out on the next roll. You'll feel like:

1. A fool;
2. You just cost your buddy fifty bucks; or
3. You don't know crap about craps.

If you remember anything from the advice in this chapter, remember this: Run like hell when someone says, "I'd just love to watch you play!" If you want to show off, your friends will be impressed all right—by how stupid you are.

7 THE FIVE MOST COMMON MISTAKES PLAYERS MAKE

I doubt if many other authors have studied the typical player as often as I have. When I began the bulk of my writings in the early '80s and again in the middle '90s, there was no question that gamblers were fraught with dubious advice—or worse, with *wrong* advice—in their quest for winning. Did I see much change in the typical player during that decade? Unfortunately, I did. Things got worse. With so many new casinos opening during that era, new players were weaned on the new trends of the time, a new generation accustomed to having everything fast and everything now. (Computers, you know.) These changes have been reflected in all walks of life, including the casino.

Clearly, patience, basic discipline and the desire to learn and study the games have taken a back seat in the "now" generation. It explains why blackjack, a skill game that needs tons of study, has flattened out in recent years. It also explains why horse racing is fast becoming a dying institution. It seems that nobody wants to study anymore. Few players exhibit the patience to wait out an opportunity.

Here is my list of the five most common things players don't know or don't do. We've already hit on the first one, knowledge.

MISTAKE #1: LACK OF KNOWLEDGE

Clearly the casino has a luxury advantage that goes far beyond its percentage advantage: Most players don't know how to play! Only a few actually bother to buy a book or read a gambling magazine. At first it surprised me, but it doesn't surprise me anymore. It would seem as if players only want to play; they don't want to learn how to play. Even the rudimentary aspects of the games escape many players. You see it best—or maybe I should say worst—at the blackjack tables.

I watched a young lady get advice from her boyfriend on how not to bust. Simply don't hit a "bust" hand. It was simple! She would stand on every hand 12 or higher regardless of the dealer's upcard. Those of you who know the cost of this abomination of the basic strategy will shudder in disbelief. But I won't. Players who lack knowledge of the games have no way of knowing what is right or wrong. We've all seen players splitting a 20 in the hope of getting two 20's, but instead they manage to convert a nearly perfect hand into two not-so-perfect hands. Is this greed or is it a lack of knowledge? Actually, it's a little of both. I know players who do this even though they know they shouldn't. No one but they themselves will be able to remedy such a mammoth problem.

In a later chapter about professional players, we'll learn that experience is one of the best sources of knowledge, which in turn breeds confidence. But not in the case of the playing mistakes I've just noted. Experience won't help if you don't learn from your mistakes. Besides, with all the mistakes our misinformed players were making, they wouldn't be able to afford any more experience to learn from!

MISTAKE #2: NOT QUITTING WINNERS

In the first chapter I introduced the term quitting winners, meaning to quit while you're ahead. But most players don't quit when they're ahead: They seem to have a destructive tendency to give back their winnings. They do it in two different ways: either slowly or quickly. I've seen players who are simply too lazy to move when a table begins to turn, so they sit there and try every conservative move they can make to stretch their money. Or in frustration, they plunk down a big bet or two (or three) in the hope of getting back in the win column quickly.

Whether you give your winnings back slowly or quickly is beside the point. It makes no difference. The opportunity that created your winnings has passed, so there's only one logical thing to do—quit. But for some reason or other, the players I'm talking about simply don't know when to quit. Or should I say they don't know *how* to quit? They don't know how to quit winners.

Would it be patronizing of me to explain exactly how one goes about quitting? It's easy. You pick up your chips and put them in your pocket. Say bye-bye to the dealer and walk away in the direction of the casino cage. Exchange your chips for cash and you will have completed the act of quitting. Now pat yourself on the back. Indeed that was patronizing of me and to show my apology, allow me to offer you a couple of solid tips that might help ensure that you always walk away a winner.

I told you a story earlier about how I hide some of my winnings in my back pocket to take that money out of circulation. Well, I actually have a scheme I follow that forces me to do this. For example, I remember the time at a dice table when I hit a come bet with an 11 and decided to let it ride in the come. Another 11 and I gave it another ride. The pile of chips moved to the 10 and I covered full odds while worrying

that my presses might now come back to haunt me. But they didn't, and I collected a whopping 800 buckeroos. The quarter bet on the come grew to $100, I added $200 in odds and pulled back a net win of $575.

Guess where that $575 went?

In another strange event at a dice table, I had my line bets and come bets well up through nearly 15 minutes of numbers and here came the dice bouncing down to my end of the table with a 3-4 staring me in the face. The 4-die landed on a short stack of chips as I was just starting to frown when miraculously, it slid off the edge of the stack and landed on a 1-spot for the shooter's point of 4! It was like slow motion. All the players at my end of the table saw the 7 and groaned; then, like magic, the 7 turned into a 4 and the table erupted!

And the winnings? That's right—all the black chips found a new home in my back pocket.

It doesn't have to be some unusual event to fill my pocket. I've been doing this for so long that it's become a matter of routine during winning sessions. If I have started a blackjack session with $40 and then work my way up to a $200 win, I'll sock $100 of that money in my pocket and play with $60, knowing that I'm going to leave that table a winner. What's really fun is checking that pocket later in the day. But now I check all my pockets since I realized that I can also slide chips into my coat pockets more easily and without calling attention to it.

Incidentally, I like to squirrel away chips for another reason: I don't want my chips on display in front of me for everyone to see. I don't want the bosses and other players around me, not to mention thieves, to see how much I've actually won. I don't like it any more than I would like someone peeking into my wallet.

MISTAKE #3: QUITTING LOSERS

Quitting winners isn't that easy, is it? And there's more to it, isn't there? Of course there is! For one, the term "quitting winners" can suggest a false sense of expectation at the tables, at the machines, at the track or at any other gambling endeavor. The term suggests there is always a time during your playing sessions when you're ahead. That would certainly make it easy: Just wait until you're ahead and then quit! But we all know there are many playing sessions where you quickly find yourself in a hole, and the longer you play the deeper it gets. You're never ahead, so how can you quit winners? Obviously you can't, so pay heed to this advice:

> A good gambler knows how to quit winners. A better gambler knows how to quit losers.

Of all the things my good friend George Nowak has told me over the years, this quote sticks in my mind. As all Las Vegans know or will eventually find out, walking away a loser is a helluva lot tougher than walking away a winner. But it's the mark of a tough player. The worst thing you can do during a particularly cold session is to keep playing, "chasing your losses" as it's called. The basic philosophy of wise gamblers is to let your winnings run and lay back on your losses. If it just isn't working for you, the best thing you can do is get away from it. For how long? If you live in Las Vegas, "long" can mean a long, long time—as measured in years. But for the rest of us, we accept the fact that we got beaten, we cut our losses, and we plan our next battle. For me personally, if I get beaten in the morning, I may very well not play again until the next morning even if I'm only on a two-day junket.

Indeed, it takes a great deal of discipline to admit defeat. The real-world analogy to all this is like putting your tail

between your legs and running away from a good fight. And that's probably the reason so many gamblers don't do it—they take the macho approach and fight like Rambo. But hey, this isn't the movies, this is the real world! And there always comes a time when the best course of action is to retreat: just ask George Custer.

MISTAKE #4: BETTING A HOT STREAK

Many years ago at the Dunes in Las Vegas before it went down in a hail of cannon fire, I had the pleasure of being one of sixteen extremely fortunate dice players to make a run at history. Actually, it was only one of us who made the mark: the shooter. And who could forget him? In every other way, he was forgettable but he got his 45 minutes of fame while the rest of us simply tagged along for the ride of a lifetime. I took a lot of "rides" at the dice tables of the old Dunes, one of my absolute favorite places to play. During its heyday, it was exactly the way I want to remember Vegas before the theme-park craze of the '90s. In the days when Vegas lived or died on gambling (read, it "flourished" because no one else had gambling), the Dunes had that great '50s look right up to its demise. The hotel stayed essentially unchanged in its later years because it simply didn't have the money to modernize. While most young visitors thought the place looked old, I thought it looked great! But I digress: When you get older, you have a tendency to do that.

To make an unnecessarily long story short, the shooter got on one helluva roll and made more numbers than I've ever seen in my life. It was clean-up city for everyone at the table and anyone who simply walked up and wanted to play. And that included me. That's right. I didn't have to worm my way in because the casino was basically dead, can you believe it?

There was actually room to get in nearly 20 minutes after he started blowing off numbers. In plain English, it was the reason dice players play—to experience the heat of the hottest of the hot shoots. Chips were piling up in front of all the players, and refills were coming by the armfuls. Eventually the table was bulging with players while a crowd formed from out of nowhere. I swear people must have come in from off the street. It was as if someone had changed the famous Dunes sign from "All-You-Can-Eat Buffet After 4 PM" to "All-You-Can-Win Craps Table Going on Right Now!"

Because the casino wasn't that busy, the yelling and screaming attracted other gamblers who were not dyed-in-the-wool dice players. Some didn't even know much about the game. (Oh, for want of a good craps book!) After the table had filled up, several players literally sold their spots at the table to other hungry and experienced players for a token $25 chip. One guy even held out for two chips and walked away like he had just robbed a bank. The player next to me knew how to play; at least he knew how to bet the pass line. That's all he was doing: no come bets, no place bets, not even a prop bet. He bumped up his line bets a little at a time, but that was about it.

"Make a few come bets," I told him. "Something like this doesn't happen very often. You should take advantage."

"No," he said. "I read where the only good bet to make is a pass line bet, so that's what I'm doing."

"That's right," I said, "but come bets have the same percentages. Make a few. Jump in!"

"No, but thanks for the tip. I'm doing just fine."

The book this guy read must have been what I call a "how-to-play" book. He knew the basic bets and he looked like the type who would have been interested in all the mathematical stuff, so he probably knew that too. But he didn't know how to recognize an opportunity. And boy, was it knocking! When the shooter finally sevened-out—and it seemed like hours, not

minutes—the casino had lost over $100,000! But it only lost a few hundred to the guy next to me.

It's like a dice dealer told me once: "The toughest part of this game is to bet heavy when the dice are passing. Most players don't bet enough during a hot streak."

Indeed you gotta know *when*. And then you gotta do it. No guts, no glory!

There's an interesting sideline to this story. When the table cleared and everyone headed for the cashier's cage, the rumblings I heard were disheartening. It was during a time when the great Dunes hotel had fallen into its worst financial trouble, and it seems that the casino had trouble coming up with the cash to pay off all the winners. A pit boss told me the hotel had just changed all of its 100-watt light bulbs to 75-watters, which explained why the casino seemed a bit dark. The Dunes had been through tough times before and it did make good on its chips; it just took a little more time to count them out to all the winners. The mad dash was like a run on the bank: No one wanted to be at the end of the line.

MISTAKE #5: THE REST OF THE WORST

It's difficult to pick the one last spot on this list. There are so many gambling sins that one would wonder if gambling itself is the biggest mistake! For many players, it is. But this book is not meant to chastise—it is meant to educate in the hope that knowledge will help my readers become better gamblers.

Problems occur everywhere you look in a casino. And in some way, they all relate to an egregious lack of discipline—the discipline to do what you know is right, and not do what you know is wrong. Playing for comps is a good example. So is being greedy trying to push small wins into big wins when the table simply won't oblige. But perhaps I see this mistake most often of all: A small, token win just doesn't cut it for most players. They simply don't understand that in the casino, you have to take what you can get.

Those who say that a casino is a microcosm of our lives are probably right. But more than anything else, the casino is a microcosm of our mistakes.

8 THE FOUR MOST VULNERABLE CASINO GAMES

Even a novice player knows that some games are better than others. If you ask a novice player which game heads the list for the best chance of success, I can almost assure you the answer would be blackjack. And that's the answer the casino would like to hear—but it's the wrong answer.

Later in this chapter, we'll learn how to identify the games that are worth your attention simply by applying a one-word test. But for now, let's review all the games, even though you may already know how to play them. Hey, a refresher course can't hurt!

CRAPS

Craps may seem to be the most complicated of all the casino games to a novice, but it's really the easiest. When the dice are coming out, a 7 or 11 wins a bet on the pass line, and a 2, 3, or 12 loses on the pass line. If one of the other numbers (4, 5, 6, 8, 9 or 10) is rolled, called a point number, that number must be rolled again before a 7 rolls in order to win the pass line. That's it. That's the basic game.

If you want to have more than one bet working for you, as most dice players do, a come bet allows you to make another bet "in the come," which is treated just like a pass line wager.

Think of it as a delayed pass-line bet. Come bets are made while a shooter is trying to repeat a point number.

You can "take odds" betting the pass line and making come bets, which is something you should always do because the casino pays odds bets at "true" odds; that is, odds that do not give the house an advantage. An odds bet is the only "fair" bet you can make in the casino. Nearly all casinos today allow you to take odds of at least double your pass line bet or come bet. Many other bets are also available, but most of them are not good bets to make. Stick to the basic game. If you didn't know the game before you read this page, at least now you know why sometimes the 7 is good, and sometimes the 7 is bad. The 7 wins on the come out, but loses when the shooter is trying to repeat a point number.

Craps is the game I play most often. Not because it's the best game to play—it isn't—but because some of my largest wins have come at the dice tables. You're probably thinking some of my biggest losses have come at the dice tables too. No, they haven't. I don't have large losses. Some people who know me actually believe I've been able to buck the odds at this game. Well, not exactly. I've been fortunate through the years without resorting to "trick shots," and you've probably known people who also seem to have had uncanny success. I stick with pass line and come bets with full double odds or triple-odds or as-many-times odds as I can get. I don't get caught up in the high-percentage bets like hardways, and I watch the game closely to make sure my betting isn't getting ahead of me. Craps is a streaky game with hot and cold runs. And that's what any good dice player is looking for—a hot streak—a streak of numbers, as many as you can see before the inevitable 7 is rolled.

This game produces what seems like the most exceptions to mathematical certainties, but only because such certainties are based on the long term. Because of the unusual short-term potential to this game, I consider craps somewhat vulnerable, but only if you're a hit-and-run type of player. If you can muster enough short-term wins—substantial ones—and your betting habits are infallible, then you might be one of the few who can win against the odds.

But don't get the idea that you can make a living at craps. It's full of pitfalls, not the least of which is an invincible force to reckon with—the casino *owns* the 7! The only players I know who might be able to defeat that edge and win consistently are mechanics who have mastered the art of throwing dice. It's inappropriate in this book to cover that interesting part of the game because I want to teach you how to win by the rules. Controlled dice shots are a form of cheating, which might come as a surprise to many dice players. If the casino catches you, you'll be treated the same way as some moron that feeds slugs into a slot machine.

If you'd like to read more about dice mechanics (for informational purposes only), may I suggest *Conquering Casino Craps*. There's a full-blown section on these guys and the incredible results they can achieve.

BLACKJACK

During the '60s and '70s, blackjack was a beatable game, no question about it. But did the casino managers simply sit around and watch their money walk out the door? I'll let you answer that one yourself. Although the game is still vulnerable to skilled players, casino countermeasures such as the infamous shuffle-up, not to mention multiple decks and deep cut-card penetration, present serious roadblocks to long-term success. Rules vary but most casinos only offer a smattering of player-friendly rules. If blackjack is your game, I'm sure I don't have to tell you that favorable rules are well worth shopping for.

Through the player options of hitting or standing, splitting or doubling, you try to build your hand without exceeding 21. That's a bust and an automatic loss, regardless of what the dealer makes. The object of the game is to beat the dealer, not necessarily to have a higher hand total than the dealer because the dealer might bust while drawing. Blackjack is far and away the most complex game offered in the casino, so pick up a copy of *Commando Craps and Blackjack* if you don't know the intricacies of the game or if you want a more detailed refresher course.

Just remember that the downside to this game is that you must draw first. It's as if you are the lead firefighter and must go first into a burning building. The dealers go in last, if they go in at all. That's why we, the valiant players, get burned more often than the dealers. Other player options can help to alleviate this huge casino advantage, although nothing can entirely eliminate it. Player options are called "basic strategy" and must be followed religiously if a player is to have any chance of escaping.

There's another strategy that players can arm themselves with. It's called "card counting," but it won't stop the roof from caving in. The casino can shuffle the cards anytime it suspects that card counters are at work, which effectively stops them cold. What's worse, the casino's cut card can cut deeply into a card counter's edge. What's the point of counting down a deck when maybe a quarter of it will never be played? And then there are multiple decks to contend with. It doesn't take a rocket scientist to figure out that removing a couple of aces from an eight-deck shoe has nowhere near the impact as compared to a single deck.

In spite of all this, most casino players play blackjack and most like it. But most lose at it, primarily because they have been duped into believing it is basically an even game and that with some fancy card counting, they can actually get a big edge. The truth is, blackjack is a dangerous game—more dangerous that the others because of the false sense of well-being that so many players have. To put it bluntly, all blackjack players think they're experts! The game is only even or better odds for a very select few players, not for every hayseed who walks up and says, "Hit me."

I'm not encouraging you to not play blackjack, and I'm not encouraging you to play blackjack or any other game of chance. If you like to play, fine. But play this game with the utmost caution.

Remember, you're a firefighter and you go in first.

BACCARAT

This stuffy game sports a very short percentage against you but like so many other games, it can only be beaten in the short term. You win, you count your money, and then you quit for life! But who does that?

The game itself is basically a coin flip: You bet on either of two hands called "player" and "banker." How the cards are dealt is a bit complicated, although fully explained in my book, *Casino Games*. I must admit there was a time when I was really involved in this game and, like so many other players, was drawn to it by the casino's "air" it puts on. Anyone can play, regardless of the casino's fluffy formality, but the minimums are generally too high for the average player. All the elaborate trappings in the baccarat pit are simply a part of the pomp the casino uses to lure the whales, the highest of the high rollers.

ROULETTE

This game doesn't head the list either, but it's far and away the most identifiable. The spinning roulette wheel has always been the signature game of casinos everywhere. Hollywood producers filming a movie in a casino always figure out a way to get a roulette wheel in the shot. It's almost become trite and unfortunately, so has the game.

There are a host of bets from picking one number out of 38 (including 0 and 00), or splitting your bet between two numbers. You can also bet a row of three, or a group of four or six or twelve. (*Casino Games* lists all the bets, payoffs, and percentages.) With one glaring exception, all the payoffs are based on the same percentages, so it really doesn't matter over the long term whether you bet one number or a dozen.

Players over the centuries have tried in vain to beat the wheel, and there have been some notably interesting assaults. Indeed there are players galore, even today, who claim the wheel is vulnerable to a host of anomalies. *Casino Games* covers them all and makes for interesting reading, but such notions as "wheel clocking" and "wheel bias" should not be the basis for risking serious money.

Roulette is a game of hope, luck and timing. It's also a game of systems. Novice players place great importance on previous numbers the wheel has churned out. In fact, players have been charting a wheel for so long that casinos today make it easy on the players by displaying the past numbers on a big lighted board right at the table. No need for pencil and paper—and no need for the board either. Those numbers have no bearing on what the wheel is about to do. But try to tell that to a novice player. Even experienced players still glance at the number board from time to time. "Hmm, I think 19 is overdue." Overdue? Try to tell a roulette player that there is no such thing.

They don't listen. They only hope.

VIDEO POKER

There are some video poker machines, particularly in Nevada, that offer progressive royal flush jackpots far in excess of the usual 4,000-coin payoff. When taken into account, these machines appear to give the player a distinct edge. But the edge is not a sure thing because the percentages are based over the full cycle of the machine, which can be staggering. It's possible, even likely, that if you play the machine 50,000 times, the royal flush will still escape you. True long-term trials are 10 to 20 times the machine's cycle, and you still have no assurance of hitting the royal.

Please don't misunderstand the term "cycle." It's a term all machine designers use, but one that is often misused by players. The cycle is simply a reference to all the possible outcomes for which a machine has been programmed; that is, all the different hands that can appear on the screen, from a garbage hand to a beautiful royal flush. Some reel-type slot machines produce cycles in the tens of millions of possible outcomes. Even though the machine might look mechanical, this is done with computer chips in order to produce jackpots in the tens of millions of dollars.

Poker machines, however, rarely offer such huge jackpots because the game is based on a true cycle of an actual 52-card deck. To make royal flush jackpots bigger than what a standard machine can offer, program designers have concocted royal flush jackpots well into the hundreds of thousands of dollars by requiring that the royal is in perfect ascending or descending order, is of a particular suit, or includes additional symbols that appear on the cards.

But as I alluded to at the top of this section, it is the progressive machines that attract experienced players, even professional teams. If one could ever say a video poker machine is vulnerable, this is the guy. The problem, as you might have experienced, is playing the machines. It's hard to get to them! Even in the wee hours of the morning, many other players are after the same thing you are. And while they play for that giant jackpot, they continue to build it even higher.

That's the idea of a progressive bank of machines, and that's the only situation in which I can honestly recommend an all-out effort. But remember, no matter how big the jackpot, no matter how many hours you try, no one can guarantee a win. True, in theory you would hit it eventually if you formed a team and tied up all the machines—but by the time it hits, you might have already spent the jackpot!

Video poker can provide decent short-term possibilities, assuming the player has shopped around for the best paytables, which are displayed right on the machine. You should also know that video poker is now recognized as one of the leading addictions of gamblers, especially women, so be careful.

RANDOMNESS

No, randomness is not a game. I'm not even sure if it's a word. But if you recall, I told you that we can identify the games worth your attention by applying a one-word test. And that's the word: *randomness.* The games we've talked about so far are purely random, at least by my definition. For the sake of this discussion, I must define "random" in a wider sense of the word, but it will help make the picture clearer. Think of a random game as one in which the decisions you are betting on are based on unbiased, uncontrollable and unpredictable events, not events that can be biased, controlled or predicted by skill.

A coin toss is random, right? But what if someone were an expert coin tosser? Would you want to wager with this guy? A coin flip is supposed to be random, but if he's an expert at it, trust me the flip isn't random. Yes indeed, there actually are people out there who can cleverly control a coin flip. How? They practice a lot. My guess is they have a little too much free time.

A better example: If we were betting on an evenly matched football game without benefit of any handicapping skill, I would consider the event essentially random because we have no control over the event as a bettor (at least we're not supposed to), and we can't really honest-to-gosh predict the winner. The choice would be essentially a coin flip (an honest one). But what if we did have benefit of expert handicapping skills? Then it isn't random! Now that doesn't mean we're guaranteed a winner, it just means we've introduced a skill to sort through all the things that made us think the game was random.

Like the coin toss, the football game only appears to be random. It's a random event for some, but for others it has a distinct predictability. For novice bettors, the factors that seem to make the game random are quite convincing. Just consider the magnitude of things that could influence the outcome: There's everything from bad officiating to missed extra points, from changing emotions to changing weather, from unexpected injuries to the seemingly uneventful coin toss. Looks pretty random, doesn't it? Surprise! Many of these things (and more) are what experts work on to actually lend some predictability to the game!

So what if we go to the other extreme where the game is a mismatch, so huge a mismatch that the outcome is a foregone conclusion? The point spread will, or at least should, effectively handicap the bias, right? Wrong! The point spread actually introduces another element to the puzzle, an element that can be carefully weighed in the hope of detecting yet another bias. I hear it time and time again: "The sports books put up the wrong number." I used the example of a mismatch because that's generally the kind of game where the point spread is more likely to be skewed. Mismatches are a favorite of expert handicappers.

I hope the picture is clearing up for you. What we're looking for is a game, even a football game, that isn't based on a purely random event like the spin of a roulette wheel. No level of expert handicapping can break through that barrier. In addition, the game must be defeatable by using skill.

All gambling events can be categorized in two columns:

1. Purely random, because they are unbiased, uncontrollable and unpredictable; and

2. Non-random, but only to those who can decipher the factors that appear random to the masses. The key is finding the games that can be defeated by skill. Those are the games listed in the column on the right in the chart pictured here. Incidentally, you can't legally change the randomness of an event, but you can defeat it. I think it's important to make that distinction.

GAME DIFFERENTIATION BASED ON POTENTIAL FOR LONG-TERM PLAYER SUCCESS	
RANDOM	**NON-RANDOM**
CRAPS	LIVE POKER
BLACKJACK (w/o counting)	SPORTS BETTING
BACCARAT	HORSE RACING
ROULETTE	BLACKJACK (w/counting)
KENO	
SLOTS	

The term *random* means a game in which the decisions you are betting on are based on unbiased, non-controllable and unpredictable events, not events that can be biased, controlled or predicted by skill.

You might think that craps is a controllable game in the sense that when shooting the dice, the players actually determine the outcome. But the shooter, unless he or she is a skilled mechanic, has absolutely no control over the outcome. The shooter creates numbers, but not specific numbers. A legal dice game is as random as a roulette wheel.

I listed blackjack as both a random and non-random game, although we know that the percentages are constantly changing. The delivery of the cards is a purely random event, which places the game clearly in the random column. The reason I did this is because the great majority of players don't know when the percentages are indeed changing. For them, the game is purely random. I see no point in adding to the glut of misinformation by listing blackjack only in the non-random column. The reason blackjack also belongs in the non-random column is simply because some players are able to lend some element of predictability to the game through card counting. The predictability factor doesn't mean a card counter can actually predict what cards will come out of the shoe; it simply means a card counter acquires a better-than-random expectation through his or her skill.

The comparison between video poker and live poker makes for an interesting discussion in terms of randomness. Clearly both games require skill for at least the chance of success but, with the exception of the large video progressive jackpots, only live poker offers a long-term chance of success with applied skill. In the case of the typical non-progressive video poker machines, players will find that their skill—although important to minimize losses—is not enough to ensure long-term consistency in winning. In other words, the element of skill is not enough to overcome the machine's percentages. The manufacturers of video poker machines take optimum skill into account when assigning a machine's percentage. If the machine is said to be a 98-percent machine—meaning it holds only 2 percent of your play on long-term average—even a player with top skill will not be able to defeat the 2-percent hold over the long term. Lesser skilled players will actually increase the machine's hold to the degree that they make wrong decisions.

Let me repeat two important things we've learned so far:

1. A purely random game with a negative expectancy cannot be beaten over the long term with skill, even though it can be beaten time and time again in the short term with only luck as your ally.

2. Games that are not entirely random are the only games that can be beaten over the long term with skill, but they might as well be purely random if skill is not applied. Blackjack is the preeminent example.

The randomness of casino games is what all casino managers count on to ensure their house PC (percentage). The randomness of the games is what every player is trying to overcome. No one wants to play when the game's decisions are following their negative expectation. When a game's negative decisions are falling neatly into place like pieces of a giant puzzle, the bosses smile, the players frown, and the casino's money is safe.

Surprisingly, the only way a player can change the randomness of a game is through some cheating scam. And that's not the way to overcome the problem. Here are a couple of things a player *can* do to defeat the randomness problem. First and foremost, play the games that are not entirely random such as live poker, horse racing or sports betting. In those games, the casino makes money through a commission of sorts—a "rake" on the poker tables, a "take-out" at the track, "juice" in the sports book. It's worth repeating that these are the principal games to play, where a skill—a *very good* skill—can produce consistent winnings, winnings that are not of any concern to the house. You could win or lose for all it cares. The house makes its money by taking a percentage of your action.

Second, when playing games based on randomness, learn how to identify a component of the game that can cause a change in randomness. For example, skilled blackjack card counters are looking for a shoe that's rich in aces and 10-value cards. They keep track of the cards played from the shoe and ascertain the construction of the remaining deck through mental gymnastics. A shoe that's constructed randomly doesn't get the job done. This advantage is so significant and unique that it's worth honing into a workable skill. As I've mentioned, the problem is twofold:

1. Casino countermeasures, including the shuffle-up, cut-card penetration and multiple decks, are nearly impossible to overcome; and

2. Card counters tend to develop an arrogance that makes them think they are unbeatable. Too many blackjack players think they have the skill required to beat the game—but most card counters aren't nearly as good as they think they are.

The only other game components I know of that might alter randomness are the selection devices that create the decisions of a game, such as the hopper in the keno lounge and the bias of a roulette wheel. But it's a long, long stretch to pull any mathematical certainty out of such claims. Even if there is bias in any of these games, chances are that it is undetectable. Fact is, at the roulette wheel, at the slot machines, in the keno lounge, and even at the dice tables, there's little that players can do to skew the games' randomness. They can only hope they've picked the right time to play when the decisions appear to defy the laws of random numbers.

At the dice tables, it's every player's goal to somehow beat that one-in-six likelihood of a 7. If a 7 doesn't appear for 15 or 20 tosses, it usually means the table will be a loser for the house; in other words, the players will win. Keeping that nasty

7 away is what hot shoots are built on. Technically, the issue of beating the odds of a 7 is based on an anomaly of events, not on the probabilities, and certainly not on the randomness of the game—but tell that to a casino manager. When the dice are passing and it seems as if there are no 7's on the dice, it's the casino's turn to get superstitious. The bosses will change the stickman prematurely. They'll stop the game to look at the dice. I've even seen a pit boss change the bowl (change the dice) in the middle of a long shoot. There's nothing worse for the pit boss than having to stand there and watch number after number. As a player-friend once told me, "Hey, I love to watch the bosses during a hot shoot. You can see the anxiety on their faces. It's the icing on the cake!"

ELM STREET

I knew a player once who was always afraid to walk away from a dice table for fear the next shooter would roll a really hot hand. He always wanted to go "just one more shooter" in case a hot hand was on the horizon. As you can appreciate, he never left the table with chips. In fact, that's the only time he left—when he ran out.

Here was a guy who harbored such terrible fears that even after he quit, he would walk back to that same table a few minutes later just to see if his worst fears were real. He had these nasty visions of walking back and seeing people stacked three deep at that same table, players yelling and screaming, "Press my 8 to $600! Press the hardways $100 each!" Freddy himself couldn't have conjured up a more terrifying nightmare.

But no. The table was just as he left it. You could almost hear his sigh of relief, but relief for only a moment. He would lie awake in his bed ten stories above the casino wondering how that same table was doing. There's a pit boss somewhere in

Vegas who could finish this story for me, the one who would get what he first thought were crank calls, though they were serious. "Hey, listen buddy, the table's still the same. Go to bed, huh."

I can only hope my paranoid friend picks up a copy of this book because I've got some enlightening news for him. In this chapter on randomness, it is indeed the randomness of the game that could save his sanity. Read on!

BUTTERFLIES

When I first began accumulating data for this book, I talked to several experts on randomness, mostly college professors including Joseph Ford, regent's professor of physics at Georgia Institute of Technology. Ford told me that the slightest change in conditions, even something infinitesimally small, will throw events dramatically out of kilter no different than you would expect from a large change in conditions. A small change, even one virtually imperceptible, can forever change the *run* of events. To make his point about the significance of otherwise subtle things, Ford said:

> "In order to be able to predict the weather three weeks in advance, say in Washington for example, that weather three weeks from now can be so unbelievably sensitive to what is going on all over the earth that to predict it accurately three weeks from now, I need to know whether a butterfly flapped its wings near Mount Kilimanjaro."

Nothing could be more analogous to this uncanny law of nature than, you guessed it, a craps table. Fate takes many paths, but you can be sure that the dice will tumble along different paths producing different decisions, depending in part upon your presence or—and this is the important part—your absence from the table! By just standing at the table, even if you are not throwing the dice, you are having a profound effect on the dice decisions. Your passing glance to the shooter catches his eye and he delays the throw just long enough to shake the dice another millisecond. Your late instructions to the dealer for a bet change slows up the game a few seconds while the dice are still rattling in the shooter's hand. And the obvious factor: Your chips on the table come in contact with the bouncing dice. And what about the player who takes your spot when you leave? *His* chips on the table and *his* actions will have the same varying effect on time and physical conditions that will forever alter the course of events.

But wait a minute! Why would you wonder what the dice are doing after you left anyhow? What difference does it make? It made a big difference to the guy in my story, and I'm willing to bet that you too have experienced similar concerns, maybe not as traumatic but concerns nonetheless. Am I right?

Right or wrong, we can all rest easy now that we know that any future change in the table conditions are subject to the most incredible whims of chance. And we might all take some relief in knowing that future hot streaks would undoubtedly not have happened had we stayed at our table. Be thankful for butterflies!

9 THE THREE TRAITS OF PROFESSIONAL PLAYERS

The most obvious stereotype of a professional gambler has to be a poker player. Of all the earmarks of a professional poker player, one distinguishing trait sticks in my mind. Even though it's easy to recognize, it's hard to define. There's an indescribable "psyche" to these pros that's hard to translate on paper. I've heard it called street smarts, but that's too common. I've heard the term grift, which is getting closer. And I've heard it described as animal instinct, which may not be the most complimentary description but it should help paint the picture.

A top poker player once told me he only has to look in someone's eyes and he can sense aggression or fear. In his own words, "The eyes tell me if I'm gonna eat or get eaten!" He calls it a "stare down," like one dog encountering another. If it just so happens that you like to play poker machines and not the live game, I agree there's no point having a stare down with a video poker machine. I doubt if even Christopher Lee's bloodshot eyes could make any machine start paying off. By the same token, I don't want to suggest you need a corner man to get you all psyched up like a boxer just before a big fight. I simply wanted you to know what that poker player told me because I believe we can find the real trait we're looking for in our analysis of this interesting tactic.

Indeed I believe that the quality we're looking for is confidence—a much more palatable quality. Confidence is

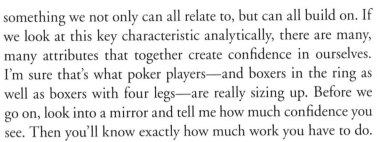
something we not only can all relate to, but can all build on. If we look at this key characteristic analytically, there are many, many attributes that together create confidence in ourselves. I'm sure that's what poker players—and boxers in the ring as well as boxers with four legs—are really sizing up. Before we go on, look into a mirror and tell me how much confidence you see. Then you'll know exactly how much work you have to do.

Here are the attributes we need to inspire confidence.

THE THREE ATTRIBUTES OF CONFIDENCE

1. KNOWLEDGE

Learn the games well and never stop learning. Knowledge is not only power, it's the hallmark of confidence. Top players know every facet of their game and of other top players. Knowledge comes mostly from experience. You learn things by just doing it (my compliments to Nike), things that you don't learn in class or from any book. Nothing can take the place of experience!

2. CONDITIONING

In my earlier writings, I made a rather controversial claim that most gamblers are conditioned to lose. And it's true. Most players actually anticipate losing. Obviously I'm talking about mental conditioning not physical conditioning, although that's important too. According to Marvin Karlins, author of *The Book Casino Managers Fear The Most,* a good gambler is both mentally and physically solid. Condition yourself to believe you can win. Then go out and do it!

3. DISCIPLINE

I've already covered many of the disciplines you'll need to be a winner. Here's a rather unique set of discipline rules that I got straight from one of the best blackjack players I've ever met. Pay heed!

1. **If you're tired, moody, frustrated or have too many things on your mind, don't play.**

   Gambling requires that all your senses are sharp. You need to be able to react quickly and correctly to an important decision—the decision to continue playing or quit. A tired or frustrated player will often make the decision to continue playing even when all the obvious signs point to quitting.

   Why?

   Perhaps it's the self-destructive nature of many people to continue doing what is clearly a mistake as a punitive measure for having made the mistake in the first place, or for not correcting the mistake sooner. Psychologists believe that most gamblers are self-destructive. I tend to agree, but I also believe the problem can be exacerbated by a dulled state of mind.

2. **If your anxiety level is too high, don't play.**

   I make it a cardinal rule never to play when I first arrive at a casino. I temper my anxiety with a preplanned meeting, a lunch, a dinner, a massage, a show, something or anything to do first. Chances are I'm tired from the trip. I may want to simply rest. At the very least, I need to get acclimated. Many times I'll schedule my arrival for late evening, which makes the next thing to do easy: go to bed.

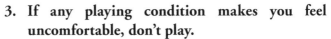

3. **If any playing condition makes you feel uncomfortable, don't play.**

It might be an unruly player, it might be the noise level, or it might be a headache coming on. It might even be something as common as an overcrowded casino. And why would a professional be so sensitive to all this? Because professionals know how important it is to start with a win! And they want absolutely nothing standing in their way.

As you now know, I'll settle for even a small win. *Any* win! My first session is that important to me. It's tough to play catch-up, but that's exactly what happens when you start off with a loss. Your first crack at the tables is by far the most important. It may very well set the tone for your entire trip. Take this to the bank: It's tough to win. It's even tougher to get even.

4. **If you harbor any negative thoughts about winning, don't play.**

If you get the slightest negative vibe at a blackjack table, don't just sit there waiting for it to go away. You go away. Don't play unless you feel totally immersed in a positive flow of energy. You'll know the feeling because it's one of confidence. And you know what confidence feels like, don't you? It feels like success. Don't ever underestimate the power of positive thinking.

It's no different from the famous story about the blackjack pro who was attending a player's banquet on the day before a big tournament. He picked up his dinner plate, his utensils and napkin, and moved to another table. He was tired of hearing some player at his table spout off about how difficult it was to win tournaments. He moved because he didn't want to be around negative people. Can you read people beyond simple smiles and frowns? Can you get an immediate sense of people who are more encouraging, more upbeat, more fun to be around? Is this really relevant, you ask? I can't think of anyplace where there are more negative people than in a casino. And like the pros, I don't want to be around them. I'm a big believer in positive association.

5. **If you don't know how to quit losers, don't play.** The first four rules tell you not to let any situation create a negative effect on your skill, your decisions, or your commonsense judgment in your quest to win, particularly during your first time at the plate. And it doesn't have to be a home run: A single will do. But what if you do strike out? And strike out again. For me and for most top players, it means an early trip to the showers. For some people, it is nearly impossible to quit winners. Can you imagine how tough it must be for them to quit losers? This rule is far and away the most important discipline to master. That's why I'm talking about it again. That's right, we talked about it before in Chapter 7. If there were some way to work it into all the chapters, I would.

It's funny how all the rules I've just listed end with "don't play." It would seem as if there are more times and more reasons to not play than to play. And there probably are, which may also explain what a retiring pit-boss friend of mine told me recently when he summed up my play over the decade I had known him: "You don't lose very often, do you, John? But then again, you don't stay put that long either, do you? It's always been hard to keep track of you."

I'd like to think he only had trouble keeping track of my losing sessions. Why? Because they didn't last that long!

SURVIVAL

Several years ago I sold a manufacturing company to a young man who has become a very good friend. We talk on the phone frequently. He's highly philosophical about business and loves to pose this tough question about the very nature of free enterprise: What should be the ultimate goal of any business owner?

Hmm. I suppose there are many answers he could get to that question: Make a profit, make a big profit, make the biggest profit possible, and so on. But no, the answer is exactly as he so profoundly believes: to survive. The name of the game is keeping the doors open. Through thick and thin you make payroll, you borrow, you find new customers, you lose old ones, you change your product, the light bulbs, and the faces around you. But one thing is a given: You are always open for business.

Think for a moment how professional gamblers deal with this problem and it will make your gambling problems much easier to resolve. Whether a sports bettor, a poker player or a handicapper at the racetrack, this "business owner" has the same real problem: He must keep playing. He doesn't have the advantage that you and I have when gambling—we can quit anytime we damn well please. But if that's the way the poker player puts food on the table, then he plays. If that's the way the track handicapper pays the rent, he plays. If that's the way the sports bettor buys clothes for his kids, he plays!

And you wouldn't believe the ups and downs. Some cold streaks can make even the most astute gambler frightfully superstitious. If he just bought a new shirt, he'll throw it away. A new car? He'll trade it in. The superstitions lead to paranoia;

he looks back at everything and everyone that might explain his torment. He may reach the point where he doesn't even think he can win anymore.

We can survive without one more day at the tables. We can quit. They can't.

DO IT IN THE DARK

The true professional gamblers I know tend to be loners. They are not the socially outgoing types of people you might expect; at least, not by my account. Most of these elite players do not like publicity. In fact, they shun interviews, even when they just won a big tournament. I suppose they might think the publicity will fatten up their heads, or they might be concerned that too much attention will result in too many interruptions at the table.

"Hey, saw ya on TV last night. Aren't you, uh, somebody?"

"Yeah, I'm somebody. Somebody who wants to be left alone!"

What strikes me strange about all this is the number of self-professed "professional" gamblers who seek the limelight by making videos, conducting seminars and even doing TV infomercials. I find this a strange irony that goes against the grain of what the pros that I know actually seek out: anonymity. For me, it raises several questions as to just exactly how professional these people really are. If they're that good, why are they hawking their picks or their surefire systems? It would seem that the only value in their picks and systems is in selling them to gullible players who think they've just found a professional who's willing to share his incredible fortunes. No, they haven't.

The true professionals would prefer that no one knows about their successes or failures. I've yet to see a true professional

bragging about a big score at the track or at the tables. I would almost have to think that a certain kind of paranoia sets in when they walk to the window with a hot ticket or to the cage with pocketfuls of chips: They are constantly looking over their shoulder.

An old gambling maxim says it best: Do it in the dark! And that, my friend, is the way professionals do it. Television is too bright for them. Unfortunately, some professionals have other attributes that we don't want to emulate. One of the most common is brought to light in the following short story.

IN THE DOGHOUSE WITH EDDIE

Let me ask you a personal question: If you are a professional in your line of work, have you ever ventured into an unrelated business and found yourself struggling, wondering why you did this new thing in the first place? I'm sure that many of you can confirm such entrepreneurial adventure, only to be cut down because you were not experienced in this new sideline. It could be anything from a physician wanting to open a restaurant to an attorney wanting to build a dog kennel. Of course, the kennel would be exclusively for pit bulls, rotweilers and dobermans (professional courtesy, you know).

Even big corporations have made this mistake in recent years, particularly in the '80s and '90s when the trend was to diversify into totally unrelated businesses. In time, most of these acquisitions were sold off as underperforming because, duh, they didn't relate well to the main business. Professional people seem to have this problem of wanting to find out if they can repeat their success in an unrelated field. Even I must admit that I've tried several different kinds of businesses over the years, only to find out that it is much more logical to stay within my specialty.

Of all the kinds of people who do this, I can think of no better example than professional gamblers. Of those I've had the pleasure of knowing, they've all had this annoying self-destructive trait. Obviously it's a trait not to copy but one to learn from. Case in point: Eddie was a good horseplayer who hung around Santa Anita. The track, you see, was his office. Then he'd pack up and move his office to Del Mar or Hollywood Park as the tracks opened and closed. He could have stayed at Santa Anita and simply watched the simulcast races, but simulcasting didn't work for him. He had to be there—wherever the trainers were, the jockeys, the owners, the horses, grooms and his betting buddies. That's where Eddie would set up shop.

On a chilly day in January, Eddie hit the Pick 9 at Santa Anita for a cool hundred grand. It was by far his biggest hit and at his age, it would surely give him added financial security for many years to come. But not Eddie—you see, Eddie also liked to play high-stakes poker. Even though Eddie was good at handicapping horses, he couldn't get a read on people. And that was a problem. Poker players were his nemesis. And they didn't have to be particularly good players to beat Eddie. In six months Eddie's money was gone. It was as if he had never written that impossible ticket!

So who won the money? All the California poker players who invited Eddie into their games won that money: "Sit down, Eddie, make yourself right at home!" Actually, home for Eddie was his wife's doghouse. And all he was trying to do was build a kennel.

10 HOW TO BET SMART: THE GOLLEHON STRATEGY

When you think about it, gambling is betting. If you don't bet, you don't gamble. So when you get right down to it, all the things we've talked about in this book—all the do's and don'ts, the disciplines, the game rules, and even the important psychological aspects of gambling we've covered—all these things actually apply to one simple act: the fine art of plunking down your bet.

To bet little, to bet big, to not bet at all: If only we could have the foresight to eliminate one of these three options—to bet little—gambling would be a cinch. If you're going to win the bet, bet big. If you're going to lose the bet, don't bet. Unfortunately, if you were so blessed with this extraordinary ability, chances are the bosses would get wise to you and show you out the door. They could only imagine that you must hail from some other planet.

Well guess what? It just so happens that the only bona fide betting strategy is more or less based on that premise: Bet when you have the advantage; don't bet when you don't. It's the underlying principle of card counting at a blackjack table. Card counting identifies the swings in advantage between dealer and player by keeping track of the cards played. In theory, you only bet when your count says that you have an advantage. Otherwise you just sit there and watch until the advantage is back in your

fold, or you leave the table. But to do this perfectly—and to get away with it—would be almost super-human.

> Bet when you have the advantage; don't bet when you don't.

Working under the assumptions that (1) not even the grungiest casino in the world would let you tie up a seat while you wait for that magic moment to jump in; and (2) none of us have any super-human powers anyway, allow me to teach you a betting strategy that might come off making you look like you do. It's a simple geometric progression made up of three sets of same-percentage increases, larger in the beginning and progressively smaller as the run continues.

This formulation was chosen to mimic both the likelihood of a win streak's continuation and the formation of sub-streaks, or "win clusters" as mathematicians like to call them. Plus, there's a computer-aided set of rules to follow for entering or exiting the strategy that's based on solid mathematical principles, not to mention common sense. Which reminds me: Please don't call this a "system." It is not a system. It is a strategy—and it comes with all the advantages that a good strategy offers

THE ADVANTAGES OF THE GOLLEHON STRATEGY

- Makes your betting virtually automatic. No different from the automatic decisions of using basic strategy at the blackjack tables.
- Works at any table game, not just blackjack.
- Ensures a big payday during a hot streak.
- Forces you to bet down or quit during a cold streak.

- Gives you out-of-the-gate protection against sudden losses.
- Offers two different schedules for aggressive or conservative betting.

THE GOLLEHON STRATEGY

THE GOLLEHON STRATEGY CHART			
	CONSERVATIVE	PERCENT OF INCREASE	AGGRESSIVE
PRE-PLAY	$2–3 Table Minimum	0%	$5–10 Table Minimum
FIRST LEVEL	5		15
	8	60%	25
	13		40
	20		65
	Any loss in this FIRST level returns you to pre-play		
SECOND LEVEL	28		90
	40	40%	125
	55		175
	75		250
	Any loss in this SECOND level returns you to $15*		
THIRD LEVEL	100		325
	130	30%	425
	170		550
	220		700
	Any loss in this THIRD level returns you to $90*		
	*Aggressive strategy. Use the corresponding value for the conservative strategy.		

OVERVIEW OF THE GOLLEHON STRATEGY

Before we go over the important rules for the strategy, let's talk a little about how the strategy works so that you understand how to use it. "TM" means table minimum and represents

your betting amount before you enter the progression. If you wish to use the aggressive strategy, begin play with either a $5 or $10 bet. Stay at that limit until one of three triggers occurs that allows you to enter the progression.

Once you have entered the progression, continue to increase your bet to the next amount listed as you continue to win. If you lose at any time during the run, the strategy's rules will dictate exactly how you respond. At no time do you continue with the progression following a loss.

Two different progressions are listed. Choose the one most suited to your comfort level. For many of you, the aggressive strategy might be too steep. I don't want to see you follow the progression faithfully for a few bets, then chicken out when the next bet is $250, for example. That might be too gutsy a move and make you feel uncomfortable. And that's not good. If you are not comfortable with any aspect of a gamble, don't do it. Perhaps through usage, queasy players will be able to disarm their fear and actually proceed farther and farther along. There is no danger in running out the progression because the increases have been carefully chosen so that if you do lose a large second- or third-level bet, your previous winnings accumulated during your climb will be relatively substantial. In the first level, however, a loss may leave you with only a break-even or a modest overall win. But that's the price you must pay if you want to have a chance for a big win without initially risking a lot of money.

> If you lose at any time during the run, the strategy's rules will dictate exactly how you respond. At no time do you continue with the progression following a loss.

Let me mention the fact that several bets in the conservative strategy are not in neat, even multiples such as $10, $15 and

$25. To keep the percentage of increase as close to the correct value as possible, some bets may need to be $8, $13 and $28. When you sit down to play, ask the dealer to give you both $5 chips and $1 chips in order to build up your bet to the correct amount. It's no big deal.

If you want to give the strategy every chance of working, follow the progression exactly. Any errors, especially in the early stages, may be greater than you think when expressed as a percentage, and may create negative compounding effects later on. Stick to the charts.

THE RULES OF THE GOLLEHON STRATEGY

The progressions are only a part of the strategy and will not work if you don't adhere to the strategy rules. Following the rules is just as important as following the progression!

1. Take a stake of $40 to the session.
2. Enter the session with minimum bets (either $2, $3, $5 or $10). This is called "pre-play." All pre-play bets are at the same minimum you have chosen. At a $2-minimum table, you will be able to choose your own minimum since any of the four pre-play bet sizes would be allowed.
3. Exit the session if you are unable to show a win of two or more units after a dozen hands of pre-play. A unit is the minimum bet you have chosen.
4. Exit the session if you lose three out of four consecutive hands, or lose three hands in a row in pre-play.
5. Exit the session if your stake drops to $20 in the aggressive strategy, or to $32 in the conservative strategy.

6. Enter the progression only after you have accomplished one of the following things in pre-play:
   a. You have won three out of four consecutive hands.
   b. You have won three hands in a row.
   c. You show a net win of four or more units.
7. Increase your bet to the next amount in the progression for as long as you win each bet.
8. Decrease your bet as follows whenever you lose in the progression:
   a. If the loss occurs in the first level, return to your pre-play minimum.
   b. If the loss occurs in the second level, return to the start of the progression ($15 for the aggressive strategy; $5 for the conservative strategy).
   c. If the loss occurs in the third level, return to the start of the second level ($90 for the aggressive strategy; $28 for the conservative strategy). The bet that follows a loss in the progression is called a "drop-down" bet.
9. If the drop-down bet wins while in the progression, continue the progression from that point. If the drop-down bet loses while in the progression, return to pre-play and follow Rules 3 through 6 for exiting the session or re-entering the progression. If the drop-down bet was made in pre-play, regardless of whether it wins or loses, stay in pre-play and follow rules 3 through 6 for exiting the session or re-entering the progression.

EXPLANATION OF THE RULES

RULE 1

Take a stake of $40 to the session.

I want you to get into the habit of starting play with a same-size stake every time. I've found that $40 seems to be a comfortable amount for most players, but if it seems too high for you, don't be alarmed about it because it certainly is *not* your loss limit. On the contrary: Rule 5 limits your loss per session to $8 if you're following the conservative strategy, or $20 if you're following the aggressive strategy. So why not start out with $20 instead of $40? Because I also want you to get into the habit of leaving a cold table with a goodly portion of your stake. It may only be psychological, since either way it's a $20 hit in the mouth, but I never want to put you in a position where you walk away with nothing.

Although the key to this strategy is protection at the outset, which means making table minimum bets and working with a modest starting stake, there are many players who just can't get interested in the game at these minimal levels. To those of you who fall into this category, I ask you: "Why do you want to take on additional risk? There's enough risk already. Why add to your burden?" Remember, the idea is to increase your wagers as your winnings mount, and, hopefully, reach the higher level of betting that can produce big results. The $40 starting stake may seem penny-ante to some, but understand its purpose. It is there to protect you from reaching into your wallet when the table is telling you to take a walk. I know several players who have used my strategy while bumping up the minimum and increasing the betting levels, and they wonder why the strategy isn't working. Well, duh! This action clearly removes most, if not all, of the strategy's value. I can't control the way players play, I can only give advice. If you want to start play with big wagers, I wish you luck. You'll need it.

The next thing you do in this situation is go to the cage and exchange your remaining chips for cash. And if you're like me, you'll record the session in your journal. Doing these things has a secondary purpose: It gives you something to do during your break from the tables. You might even want to get a cup of coffee and plan your next session. Personally, I keep my betting money in $20 bills, which makes it easy to find the stake to start a new session. I pull out two twenties, tell the dealer "All red," and I'm ready to go. This is an important discipline to follow, so allow me to repeat it: Always cash in your chips when you exit a session. Always begin a session with cash.

If you have won a considerable amount of money from prior sessions, lock up your money—literally. Most casinos offer safety deposit boxes at no charge to you. Never carry large amounts of cash on your person. Another advantage of using a safety deposit box is to keep you away from your winnings! I hate to see players risking more than just a small portion of their winnings for stake money.

RULE 2

Enter the session with minimum bets (either $2, $3, $5 or $10). This is called "pre-play." All pre-play bets are at the same minimum you have chosen.

Determine whether you're going to use the conservative or aggressive strategy. Note that each strategy requires a specific bet size in pre-play: $5 or $10 for the aggressive strategy, and either $2 or $3 for the conservative strategy. Remember that all bets in pre-play should be at the same amount, although there's nothing wrong with moving up from $5 to $10 in pre-play, or dropping down from $10 to $5 as the conditions warrant. The same can be said for the $2 and $3 bets for the conservative bettor, although the $1 difference in bets would not be as significant. However, for the sake of defining a "unit," the lesser of the two minimums is your unit. If you have selected a $2-minimum table, you will be able to use any of the four choices for a minimum bet. Obviously you can't bet $2 or $3 at a $5-minimum table. If $2 is all you want to bet in pre-play, and $5-minimum tables are all you can find, do not play. Don't let the casino lure you into betting more than you want to. Stick to your guns!

RULE 3

Exit the session if you are unable to show a win of two or more units after a dozen hands of pre-play. A unit is the minimum bet you have chosen.

This is the first of the three exit rules that guard against early losses or what could be regarded as poor table conditions. If you're playing at a $2-minimum table, exit the table if you have not won more than $4 (two units) over the course of a dozen hands. At a $5-minimum table, watch to see if you are up at least $10 after the dozen plays; if not, exit the table. Remember that at a $5-minimum table, you can only play the aggressive strategy.

A neat way to keep track of how many hands you have played is to simply take a chip and select a printed spot on the face near the edge to use as a "hand" position on a clock. As you play a hand, simply rotate the chip one "hour." Start with the spot at one o'clock and rotate it through the hand positions to "midnight," your twelfth hand.

RULE 4

Exit the session if you lose three out of four consecutive hands, or lose three hands in a row in pre-play.

This exit rule protects against the possibility of getting beaten by negative streaks. We're looking for hot streaks not cold streaks, so keep a keen eye on losses that seem to gang up on you. Why take the risk that these cold streaks will only continue? If such cold streaks develop late within the first dozen hands, you'll most likely have more than one reason to exit the table. It's not unusual for all three exit rules to trigger at the same time. When I encounter such poor table conditions, I won't return to that table for the rest of the day. Period.

RULE 5

Exit the session if your stake drops to $20 in the aggressive strategy, or to $32 in the conservative strategy.

This exit rule is simply to guard against an indiscernible trend. Dice players call this condition "choppy." What it really means is that the game is beating you so slowly that you don't realize it. Stop the trend at four units. And don't be concerned that you are exiting tables too frequently as you apply rules 3, 4 and 5. You will definitely find that there are more times than you imagined when the rules tell you to quit. What you'll be doing is something you probably never did as often as you should have—you're restricting your losses!

RULE 6

Enter the progression only after you have accomplished one of the following things in pre-play:

    a. You have won three out of four consecutive hands.

    b. You have won three hands in a row.

    c. You show a net win of four or more units.

Finally we get out of pre-play and start the progression. The conditions that trigger rule 6 are all positive. Winning three out of four consecutive hands is definitely a good sign. Winning three hands in a row is even better. And if ever you're up four or more units, what better time to start your assault?

RULE 7

Increase your bet to the next amount in the progression for as long as you win each bet.

This is the fun part! If you're playing the aggressive strategy, start the progression at $15. As long as you win, proceed to the next bet. If you are fortunate enough to have caught a streak that takes you through the first four-bet level, you will be ahead to the tune of at least $160, depending on your pre-play standing when you entered the progression. As you can appreciate, most of the time the progression takes you only into the first level. But do yourself a big favor: Take it as far as the consecutive wins will go. Don't be nervous. Enjoy the ride up!

RULE 8

Decrease your bet as follows whenever you lose in the progression:

    a. **If the loss occurs in the first level, return to your pre-play minimum.**

    b. **If the loss occurs in the second level, return to the start of the progression ($15 for the aggressive strategy; $5 for the conservative strategy).**

    c. **If the loss occurs in the third level, return to the start of the second level ($90 for the aggressive strategy; $28 for the conservative strategy). The bet that follows a loss in the progression is called a "drop-down" bet.**

Yes, all good things do come to an end at some time. This rule protects you from doing something stupid like continuing the progression after a loss. There's an old gambler's maxim that certainly applies here: Never press a loss. The term "press" means to double the amount of your previous wager in the hope of both winning the bet *and* making up for the loss. Indeed, the right move is to reduce your bet with a "drop-down" wager, and that's what Rule 8 tells you to do. Your next bet following a loss in the progression is reduced in proportion to the size of your losing wager.

Some players elect to exit the table after a losing bet that ends a lengthy progression. Let's say they were at $125 when they lost the bet: They can't bring themselves to cut back, so they quit. While quitting is far superior to continuing the progression, the smarter choice is to follow Rule 8 and simply cut back. With all the success you've just had, it's possible that the loss was just a blip in your future, and you may be headed back up again.

RULE 9

If the drop-down bet wins while in the progression, continue the progression from that point. If the drop-down bet loses while in the progression, return to pre-play and follow Rules 3 through 6 for exiting the session or re-entering the progression. If the drop-down bet was made in pre-play, regardless of whether it wins or loses, stay in pre-play and follow rules 3 through 6 for exiting the session or re-entering the progression.

This interesting rule covers all scenarios following a drop-down bet. If you lose the drop-down wager, it means you lost two bets in a row and you are relegated to pre-play again. If you were only in the first level when you experienced your first loss, your drop-down wager was already in pre-play. Follow Rules 3 through 6 for exiting the session or re-entering the progression.

If you win the drop-down bet while in the progression, continue with the progression at the next amount directly higher than the drop-down bet. For example, if your first loss in the aggressive progression was $90 (in the second level), your drop-down bet will be $15. If you win the drop-down bet, your next bet will be $25.

Nothing says you can't quit instead of returning to pre-play or making a drop-down bet. If you want to quit, quit! In fact, quit any time you want to, although I can't understand why anyone would want to quit while riding a nice win streak.

Most often, if players elect to quit on their own (not being forced to quit by rule), it's usually at that moment when they otherwise would have been relegated to pre-play. But if you feel like playing some more, follow the pre-play rules and see if you can re-enter the progression. If pre-play doesn't work out and you're forced to exit the session, go outside and get some fresh air. It's probably time for a break anyhow.

THE GOLLEHON STRATEGY Q & A

Q: What if I leave the table after my first loss in the progression? Do I start with a drop-down bet when I decide to play again?

A: No. When you leave the table you have ended that session. When you decide to play again, you'll be starting a new session in pre-play.

Q: Why only a $40 stake? I'd rather start with $100.

A: There's no reason to start with that much money. You won't lose all of your $40 if you follow the rules. But more important, if the playing conditions were so poor that you did lose to the strategy's limit, why would you want to risk more by starting another session right behind it? What part of the word *quit* don't you understand?

Q: If I have had success with the conservative strategy, is there anything wrong with going to the aggressive strategy the next time I play?

A: Nothing at all. You are simply progressing from one progression to the other. The idea of my strategy is to systematically make progress in your winnings by taking advantage of favorable table conditions. If you are a basic conservative bettor who ventures up to the aggressive strategy from time to time, my suggestion is that you begin future sessions in the conservative mode—at least until the time you are totally comfortable beginning at the aggressive level and are fully prepared to follow it through.

Q: I like to play with just red chips. When the progression is working, the stacks can become unwieldy. I suppose I should change over to green chips, right?

A: Absolutely. Reread my section in Chapter 3 about changing color as a way to increase your bets when you're winning. It's a natural for the strategy too. There are obvious levels in the strategy that call for a color change but more than that, it just makes it easier to manage. Go to green chips when you're in the $50 range; black chips when you're around $200. Of course, you'll still have to "mix 'n match" because the betting amounts are not in exact color multiples.

Q: I play your strategy often but find that most of the time I never get out of pre-play, so I'm stuck at the table-minimum level. Am I doing something wrong?

A: Probably not. On average you'll enter the progression only once or twice out of five typical 20- to 30-minute sessions. The time you allot to a session (other than as determined by the rules) is up to you, but you know how I feel about that. I like to keep my sessions short and sweet. If I find that I'm moving in and out of pre-play too often, only toying with the first level—or worse, fighting hard to avoid the exit rules—I may very well make a decision to exit the session regardless of the rules. Why fight it? Why not look for an easier battle?

But getting back to your question, if you don't get out of pre-play very often, it means that the table conditions were poor and you should be thankful you were "stuck" at the table-minimum level. Some players seem to think of pre-play as a penalty box. It's not! Think of it as a "protection box."

Q: Is there another progression you can write that starts with higher minimum bets so that I can get to a higher level sooner?

A: When I play craps, I use a modified version of this strategy that incorporates two stages of pre-play. In addition, the progression is considerably more aggressive to better fit the concept of that particular game. To make pre-play fit the progression, it was necessary to increase the pre-play minimums and add the additional stage. I don't want to go into that strategy now for a host of reasons, not the least of which is the fact it is geared to one particular game. Because the strategy, which I call "Power Betting," introduces higher betting levels throughout, I'm not comfortable detailing it here without considerable explanation. And this just isn't the time or place.

To simply start the Gollehon Strategy with higher minimum bets, as you suggest, would defeat the idea of protecting yourself right out of the gate. Besides, the early stages of the progression must have the correct mathematical relationship to pre-play minimums. Remember that pre-play is for your protection against continuing losses. The progression is for protection too—protection against missing out on a nice win streak. But you have to wait for it to happen!

Your question, incidentally, suggests to me that you might be just a tad greedy about all this, and I have the feeling you are a good example of someone who should not be experimenting with higher betting levels. Let's not be in too big a hurry. You need to have patience if you're going to be a good gambler. Remind me not to take you fishing with me.

Q: What if I lose while in the third level of my progression, win the $90 drop-down, but lose the next? Then what do I do?

A: It's covered in Rule 8 but I don't mind answering it again because it's important. Even though you won the drop-down bet, you've still lost two relatively large wagers. It would be foolhardy to risk another one. If you wish to continue the session, you must drop down again to $15. Since you were at $125 when you lost your second large bet, that's in the second level so you must follow Rule 8 and drop down to the beginning of the progression ($15).

Q: What are the odds of winning in a row like that? Just give me the first level.

A: Sure. The raw odds are exponential, so you can take it as far as you wish. But you must remember that our strategy takes much more than odds into account. Football bettors will quickly see why it is so difficult to pick four out of four winners, and then wonder why they are paid off at only 10 or 11 to 1 odds!

Assuming a fair game, these are the odds:

WINS IN A ROW	ODDS OF WINNING
2	3 to 1
3	7 to 1
4	15 to 1

Q: How do the different game percentages affect the likelihood of streaks?

A: Good question. Since the overall percentages are working for the house, they are obviously working against the player: *for* a losing streak and *against* a win streak. It was difficult to factor such percentages into our strategy because some game percentages vary, not to mention the games with a slew of different percentages. Dice and blackjack are good examples. There are many different bets at a dice table with percentages that vary from less than 1/2 percent to 16 percent. And blackjack is a game with constantly changing percentages.

To make the matter all the more a chore to account for, these percentages also play havoc with streaks. For example, the likelihood of winning 15 out of 30 hands of blackjack is not the same as winning 5 out of 10 hands or 1 out of 2. The accumulative effect of the game's percentages can be dramatic over a higher number of plays.

Q: What about games where I make more than one bet at a time, like roulette or dice? How do I apply this strategy?

A: Another good question. A roulette player is faced with the temptation of making several bets at one time to increase the likelihood of picking a winning number. But the percentages are constant, in spite of the apparent increase in the odds of winning. Proving this fact is simple to do: Just cover all the numbers with identical bets and see what happens. You will win for sure, but your win will be less (by two-unit bets) than the total of all your losing wagers. There really is no benefit to making multiple bets other than just hurrying along the inevitable.

My strategy is more suited to games with even-money bets such as blackjack and baccarat, but it can be used at roulette if you are making single even-money bets such as odd-even or red-black. Most of the players I know who consider themselves to be good roulette players (whatever that means) make only these bets because they consider the odds of winning to be more realistic. But with the exception of the 5-number inside bet, the percentages are all the same and there is a decision on each spin.

At the dice tables, there isn't a win-lose decision on each roll; therefore, many players also like to make multiple bets. The concept of making several smaller bets instead of one larger bet at a dice table is dubious at best, since the game percentages are working three times as hard to beat you with three bets in jeopardy instead of one. The reason this idea of multiple-bets is more costly to the player at craps than at roulette is because there are more rolls in which the bets are subject to the percentages, whereas there is only one spin at the roulette table.

If you are a multi-bet dice player, you can apply the strategy—but understand that a $5 pass-line bet and two $5 come bets all with double odds put your total wager (your exposure) at $45. Since line bets and come bets are really all that I should recommend you do, it makes it tough to bet at pre-play minimums, especially since most casinos offer nothing less than a $5-minimum table. And it's especially hard to do when we all know that you really must take full odds.

To use the strategy for craps, you'll have to devise your own pre-play minimum. And you must count the total of all bets in order to properly follow the progression. If you're fortunate enough to play in Nevada, you should be able to find $2 and even $1 tables. That will certainly help, but regardless of where you play, heed my advice at the dice tables: Keep it under control!

Q: Someone told me I've got a better chance of catching streaks at a dice table than at blackjack. Is that true?

A: According to our computer plays, yes. In fact, the likelihood of streaks appeared to be greater for craps than for any other game except baccarat. The reasons for this are no doubt inherent to the game's basic design—a "built-in" streak based on that one-in-six likelihood of a loser 7. Everyone expects at least a mini-streak of numbers before that dreaded 7 clears the table. If there actually is a likelihood for greater streaks, cold streaks would be more likely to occur—a result of the game's negative expectation.

Q: Is it okay to round off some of the bets in your strategy—say $100 instead of $90—so that it's easier to remember?

A: Let me answer your question by telling you how a blackjack counter answered the same question when I posed it over 25 years ago. While watching a very good card counter ply his trade by making all kinds of strange-sized bets, I asked him why he didn't just bet a nice, round $20 instead of the $19 he had put out in the circle. He turned around and snapped at me, telling me in no uncertain terms to mind my own business. He was faithfully following his own betting strategy that called for $19 not $20. "If the dealer doesn't like it, that's tough," he said. "If you don't like it, who cares? And if you're gonna stand there jibber-jabbering, I would prefer that you go bother someone else!"

Q: Can I combine this strategy with a count strategy at blackjack?

A: Probably not. The exception might be that rare time when the deck is running far into the player's favor and, not surprisingly, the player is on a win streak. At the beginning of this chapter, I poked a little fun at card counters because they always seem to come off a bit arrogant, as if they went to blackjack school at Harvard or something. I've always believed there is a major flaw in their counting strategy that I alluded to earlier. Basically, why sit at a table making small bets, waiting for the edge to swing, while the edge might be several percentage points against you? Most do this. Few actually leave the table. Strange.

Q: Can I make a copy of the strategy and take it with me to the blackjack tables?

A: You should be able to, but ask a pit boss before you sit down just so you don't embarrass yourself. Bosses do not want you to have anything with you that might help you count cards. Basic strategy cards are usually okay, because that really isn't card counting. In the same sense, a copy of my strategy should be okay too.

In case you can't take the copy with you, it's easy to memorize. After using it for several trips, I'm sure you won't need it anyhow. You may only need to freshen up on it at home before you leave for the casino. Nonetheless, feel free to make a photocopy of the chart. Although the chart is copyrighted, you may make a copy for your own personal use. Please don't tear the page out of the book.

Q: Is there any betting strategy that works over the long term?

A: I wish! If that were the case, we could all quit our jobs and gamble for a living. Most betting strategies are geared to short-term play. In the very short term, game percentages are not that significant in the sense that virtually anything can happen. You could easily win 10 hands in a row; you could easily lose 10 hands in a row regardless of who has the edge.

Technically, the impact of game percentages, even those that seem minuscule, can be felt at any time. But it's in the long term—an accumulation of session upon session—where those percentages always meander back to the house. One of the many ways of detecting this unwavering characteristic is to see it at work in short-term play, even while you are using the strategy. I call it "win-nine-lose-ten," which is what we are most often faced with.

The strategy protects you as best it can against continuing losses, and signals a time when it seems opportune for the birth of a streak. But the past doesn't ensure the future. The shrewd player will do as I do: Treat choppy table conditions as a down streak and quit the session. That's yet another reason why I jump from table to table so often. I'm a streak player, particularly at the dice tables—a long streak of numbers is what I'm looking for.

But unlike most other players, I have a better reason to look for it: I know what to do when I find it. The question is: How long will it last?

11 MY MOST PERSONAL ADVICE TO YOU

We've covered a lot of ground in exposing the secrets that casinos don't want you to know. You now have fewer things standing in your way of winning, but there are a few other things I want to talk to you about that are just as important. And I want to tell you about them in stories that are a bit personal in one way or another. Remember that crystal ball we used in Chapter 2? Of course, there really wasn't a crystal ball in the story; it was just theoretical to help make an important point. But sometimes I wonder if maybe I do have a crystal ball to peer into—and if maybe everyone who bothers to look has one too.

THE SIXTH SENSE

It was a Sunday morning at the Las Vegas Hilton. Our yearly January vacation to California and Vegas was coming to an end. Even though we had been there for nearly two weeks, I was still getting up early in the morning as if it were Eastern time. On this particular morning, I had the coffee shop at the Hilton pretty much to myself: The newspapers weren't in yet so I just sat there over coffee pondering what to do with my last day of gambling.

My play at the dice tables had been less than spectacular, so I had to be careful. I was down $1,000 for the trip, but I did want to get one last shot at them, so I made up my mind before I came downstairs from my room that I was going to play ultra conservatively, doing everything possible to make my last $200 stretch. Some players might have decided to go for broke (even when they were already broke) and try to force the dice. But I believe in "staying power," the term I use to describe the typical conservative way I begin betting.

And speaking of terms we've learned in this book, remember "good aggressiveness?" It's always something I look forward to using, but not on this trip apparently, as the going had not been good. My sessions at the tables were unusual in that I rarely veered from my conservative pre-play betting. Why? Because there was little reason to. Had I bet aggressively throughout the sessions, I'd be living in a cardboard box!

What was also remarkable about this particular trip were some rather strange cases of gut instinct at work. I use the term gut instinct as opposed to ESP, because I don't want you to get the idea I'm allergic to kryptonite. I don't have super powers. I simply have trained myself to listen to my instinct. And at the coffee shop of the Hilton hotel that morning, it was screaming at me. In fact, I envisioned exactly what I was going to do that morning, complete with useless details. I knew exactly which table would be operating that early, how many players would be there, and where I would stand. The only thing that didn't make sense was the image of a chaotic shoot, because I knew there were only two players for me to find. Was I "seeing" the wrong casino?

I finished my coffee and headed to the dice tables. When I got there, it was exactly the way I had seen it. There was a player at one end of the table and another guy standing beside the stickman carrying on a conversation with the pit boss. Basically he was shooting some bull; he showed little enthusiasm for shooting numbers. The whole scene had that typical "chill" look that every dice player can recognize.

I stood where I envisioned myself—at the other end of the table—a spot where I would otherwise never stand. (I like to be nearest to the center of the table, beside the stickman, so I can see the dice better at either end of the table.) The dice were pushed in front of me—it didn't take long—and I began with a modest pass line bet of $5. My point was 6 so I backed it up with $10. With a nickel riding in the come, I threw the dice hard and scored with an easy 6. The other two players at the table applauded. They told me that it was the first pass since 5:30 a.m. It was now 7:30. Obviously, they forgot some or maybe it just seemed like it.

Or maybe it really was that bad!

One pass does not make a great shoot, so I plunked down another red chip and fired the dice again. Seven. Another chip on the line. Seven. Okay, three chips on the line. Nine. Then 9 right back. I just didn't feel it, though, and I continued to make modest bets. Another few rolls and I sevened out. Did you think I was going to bore you with another one of those hot-shoot stories? Well, not quite yet.

The other players at the table (one more had joined us) were terrible. And then I turned terrible too. This went on for at least an hour and I had thoughts about finding my wife, checking out, getting in the rental car, and heading for the airport early. But I still had my stake; in fact I had almost all of it (remember, I was betting conservatively). Anyone who would have walked up and played aggressively would have been eaten alive. Indeed, this was a time not to play.

The dice made their way around the table like a racecar running many, many laps. Now here they were back to me again. I decided to throw them hard. Very hard. I rarely do that, but a little dice abuse seemed like the appropriate thing to do. I suppose I was also a little moody and perhaps upset with my play, particularly that I would even stay at the table. But I knew I had to stay. I just knew it. Any other time I would have been gone after the first few minutes, if not to another table, then to another casino or to another game.

But not this morning.

I began throwing the dice so hard they were bouncing off the table. And I was picking them up and throwing them as quickly as I could. It became a fast game because no one was making prop bets that usually slow up the game. All my comes had filled up the numbers and I had a nice run of "off and on." Things were looking up. I hit my point and remember looking at the guy at the other end of the table and winking at him. And that's something else I don't do. Either of two things will happen: One, he'll think I'm a little strange, or two, he'll want to buy me a drink. Fortunately, with the rash of numbers I had just thrown, I don't think he even paid attention.

It wasn't that I hoped I would throw more numbers. It was that I knew I was going to throw more, many more. The table began filling up like a good table will, and I quickly went from red to green chips and put two quarters on the pass line. I threw the dice hard and I threw them fast, and quickly worked my way to black. Soon I had converted most of my comes to place bets and buy bets on the 4 and 10.

Throw 'em hard, I kept thinking, but I don't know why. The dice fell on the floor so many times I think I set a house record. The other players complained and took their bets down. "Off on this roll only," they would clamor—but not me. I raked in payoffs on every toss. There were no 7's. Of course not: For me, there were no 7's on the dice!

It was 9:33 a.m., nearly 40 minutes later when I saw my first and last 7. I cashed in a little over $12,000. Sure, it could have been $112,000, but it took the guy with a sledge hammer a little too long to get to me. I didn't keep playing after the seven-out because of two reasons: I had accomplished what I had wanted and the guy at the other end of the table winked at me. I left in a hurry. It was a great ending to a most unusual trip that generated a lot of notes for this book.

I had played for three days at the usual places I liked to go: Palace Station, Desert Inn, Caesars, Bally's, Gold Coast and the Hilton. My recordkeeping for the trip turned out to be rather haunting, and I want to share some of my notes with you. Arriving at the Palace Station to meet local friends, I wrote: "I wish we could be meeting somewhere else. I'm not comfortable here anymore." I lost $300. But we had a nice lunch.

At Bally's, I lost a C-note, but my scribbling tells the story: "Feels like another loser." It was. But I had to see an old pit-boss friend of mine who was heading to a poker club in California. At Caesars, I noted on the $500 win that I was plain lucky. Actually I had played poorly, and was fortunate to catch a brief but impressive hand. I left quickly thereafter.

While I was in the Hilton's race book, I had a strange premonition about a horse from a track I rarely ever bet. I put $100 on her nose and she won by 10 lengths. Someone else must have had a nudge on this little filly because she quickly came down from 12 to 1 to 5 to 1, but I happily collected. It calmed my wife because she was upset that I would do something "so stupid." For that trip, it would be the only bet I would make in the race book. Most unusual.

I told my wife which poker machine to play because she was having bad luck. Within minutes, she had filled up two buckets with quarters, and I got at least two kisses out of that. I was looking for a wink. When we first got in, I set up a golf match for the weekend with some of the guys who distribute my books for me in Vegas. But even though the forecast was okay, I canceled the round that evening. The next day, Vegas had one of the worst windstorms in history.

Out of all the hours I spent at the dice tables that fateful trip, only once did I bet aggressively. And I just told you that story. For all the other times, there simply wasn't much "feeling" to do so. And as it all turned out, with one exception, there was no reason to. Perhaps the best example was at the Desert Inn. I went there by myself just to see the place again since I hadn't stayed there in quite a while. It was pretty dead for a weekend and the vibes I got were as dead as the casino. The message rattled my guts. I played a little and left early. I had no chance. I was absolutely convinced of that the minute I walked in.

What I'm telling you about is not superstition. I hate superstitions. The last time I picked up a penny, my horse came in sixth. I simply don't subscribe to silly superstitions, but I do wholeheartedly believe in my instincts. When I gamble, I take along my most trusted friend. I never gamble with a fool.

What some people can do with their minds is beyond belief. Why most people don't even try is more amazing. This most tantalizing issue has always fascinated me and became the subject of an entire chapter in John Alcamo's *How To Avoid Casino Traps!* The chapter titled "The Mental Edge" deals primarily with memory experts, including a guy who has memorized 31,000 digits of pi. John interviewed a lot of people who had an incredible power of memory, but he didn't do much with prognosticators other than some joker he met who wanted to sell him the winner on Monday Night Football. That's not the kind of prognosticator he was looking for! And he's not entirely sure there even is such an animal, but if there is, John didn't find him.

But I'm sure of one thing: If a guy can memorize 31,000 digits of pi (3.14159…..), our brains must be able to do things we haven't quite figured out yet. Don't discount anything. Whether it comes from your guts or from your brains, go with your instincts because it's what separates us from robots. Without it, I would feel alone. We all rely on it a lot more often than we think. And for me, it works a scary number of times.

But it isn't scary. I count on it every day. I would be scared without it!

CASINO CHECKLIST

The last two decades of the twentieth century produced incredible changes in the gaming industry. Many would argue that the proliferation of gaming throughout the country only made things better for serious gamblers. I would certainly be one to take issue with that notion. Since you have so many options available to you today, deciding where to play is not easy. And it's not a decision you should make carelessly either. Where you play is just as paramount to winning as the way you play, because where you play directly affects your entire mental state—you're either comfortable or you're not, no different from a football team playing on its home turf compared to an unfamiliar field.

But can you be comfortable if the casino deals a bad game? Of course not. Simply translated, that means that if the casino just an hour or two away from your home does not offer the same great game you're accustomed to in Vegas, for example, it makes absolutely no sense to hop in the car, drive merrily along thinking about all that airfare you're saving, get there, get clobbered, and then drive home thinking about all that money you just lost because you got suckered into a bad game.

And it isn't just blackjack. Let's say you're a video poker player and let's use the same nearby casino as an example. You're walking up and down the aisles looking at the paytables. You're amazed that the machines are only 5-6's—and everyone's playing them. You can't even find a machine available! You want the 6-9's like you expect in Vegas, but there aren't any. Are you going to be suckered into playing these high-percentage, low-

payout machines? I hope not: I hope you're not that desperate to play!

If we're just going to target craps, certainly the venue plays only a small role in where you play because this game has become remarkably standardized from Nevada to the gambling boats in Florida. If you live near Atlantic City, for example, it makes little sense to spend five hours in the air, not to mention the airfare, as you head for Las Vegas. Personally, I'm never comfortable after five hours in the air, no matter where I touch down. And I don't exactly relish the thought of five more hours in the air going home.

If you live in the Midwest where riverboats have become commonplace, the boats might be the best choice for you. The same can be said for many Indian casinos that have sprouted up. Some are quite impressive but many are small and unable to accommodate their customers, especially on weekends and holidays. For many players, the confines of riverboats and small Indian casinos, as opposed to the sheer size of the MGM Grand in Vegas is a bit too… well… confining.

Until recently, I always answered the question, "Where should I play?" with this reply: "Where you win!" It made sense and it still does, sort of. Simply play where you win. But in reality, that response is a bit too simplistic, and too many players probably thought I was trying to brush them off with that succinct answer. Of all the things to consider when choosing a casino, I now have a new item to add to my list that plays a big role in determining my own comfort index. And unfortunately, it's a sign of the times.

A trusted friend of mine, a retired banker who felt very safe in a big Atlantic City casino, found out just exactly how safe he wasn't! After hitting the tables for $10,000, he went to the cage to pay off a small marker and pocketed a cool $7,000. He rolled up the bills and put a rubber band around them. He was on top of the world as he headed for the Sands next door to try to turn the seven grand into seventy grand. He never got the chance. Just outside the door, at nine in the morning—*in the morning,* mind you—someone stuck a gun in his back and told him to hand over the roll. Another man joined him to make sure the "transaction" took place smoothly. In seconds, the men were gone and so was the roll of seventy $100 bills.

Obviously, someone had been watching as my friend made his killing at the tables, and was watching as he cashed in his chips. He was marked and he still carries the mark. He's constantly looking over his shoulder; he's keenly aware of who's around him; and most important, he now stores the bulk of his winnings in a casino safety-deposit box. Incidentally, if you are ever carrying large sums of money to your room or to your car, ask at the casino security desk for an armed guard to escort you.

So have we covered it all?

Not quite. Once you've chosen the casino, you next have to choose the table. Do as I do: Watch the action at a table before you join in. But which table is worth watching? I pick a table based on the players, noting their mood and particularly the number of chips in front of them. It's not hard to size up one player's success; but I'm not looking at just one player, I'm looking at the entire table. Once I've found the table worth watching, my stake out might last for several hands. It's not a matter of being sure. I can't be sure of anything except one thing: I'm not going to plop myself down at a losing table.

This practice of mine—table watching—can be so consuming that anyone with me becomes annoyed at my waiting game, which is another reason why I like to play alone. As I walk around a casino or stand watch over a table, I simply don't feel that driving urge to play that most people feel. And that's good. I don't have an urge to play—I have an urge to win!

It's the winning part of playing that everyone likes. And for me, patience almost always helps me find it.

A PRIVATE GAME

When I get back from a trip to Vegas, Atlantic City or an Indian casino in my home state, I have to return phone calls from my friends asking, for all intents and purposes, one basic question: "Hey John, how did you do?" Frankly I don't like people asking me that. It's like asking, "How much did you pay for your car?" My stock answer to that how-did-you-do question is, "I broke even." Sure, breaking even is like kissing your sister and it probably doesn't do my reputation any good, but it's an answer. And it's all anyone is going to get from me. My financial affairs—and gambling is indeed "financial"—are nobody's business but my own.

However, what amazes me even more is how people find out about my trips. "So-and-so saw you there," is the most frequent response. If I have taken off on a business trip with a side trip to a nearby casino, it's hard to hide. "Your assistant said you were gone for a few days. Where'd ya go, Vegas?" My answer is always "Cleveland." You wouldn't believe how many trips I took to Cleveland last year.

Recall from Chapter 9 that true professional gamblers "do it in the dark." Gambling, that is. For the most part, they are private people who share little about their successes or failures. Obviously, you and I don't have to be a professional in order to take advantage of their wise traits. I've learned a lot from them and so can you.

When I play, I like to play alone. I want no one outside my family to know where I am. You'll be surprised how much better you play once you understand exactly how personal—and private— gambling really is. What works for me doesn't work for everyone else, so when my friends get back from a gambling trip, who do you suppose is the first one they call?

Read on.

THE BOTTOM LINE

How many times has someone called you and said, "Hey, I just got back from Vegas, and let me tell you about a hot hand I had." Then he spews off about the ten grand he won while he held the dice for 30 minutes.

"Okay, okay, Marty, but how did you do for the trip?"

"Huh? Oh yeah, well, the morning we left I played for about an hour and hit 'em for another three thou."

"Yeah, but how did you do for the trip?"

"I gave a little back."

"You gave a little back? What the hell does that mean? You've got thirteen thousand in winnings you're telling me about, and you gave a little back? How much back?"

"Oh, I don't know, I'm all right."

"So, how did you do for the trip?"

"Umm, I lost a few thousand."

"How many thousand?"

"Two or three."

"Too bad."

*****

"John! Guess what! I hit the trifecta last night for $300!"

"Great! So how did you do for the night?"

"Lost a couple hundred."

"You lost a couple hundred? What's the big deal about hitting the trifecta if you ended up losing a couple hundred?"

"Hey, that trifecta was nice!"

Of all my friends who gamble, it's a rare bird who cuts to the chase. I get calls all the time from my horse-playing friends, and craps shooters and sports bettors telling me about a portion of their action; obviously, only the good part. It's human nature to rationalize the losing part with the winning part or simply with the great fun one had. "Hey, we had a great evening!"

Forget the trifecta, forget the hot hand, forget the Bills' win when they came back in the second half and turned that losing ticket into a winner. What about the other football game that Sunday afternoon? Did you forget about the one you lost? Win one and lose one and you're upside down for the juice. I want to know how you did when all things are taken into account. Actually, I don't. It's not my business. I've now learned not to ask that same question that I don't like. I just listen. Sure, I like hearing about the nice wins as much as anyone. I'm win-oriented. I want to hear about people winning, but I want to make sure you don't make the same mistake.

Don't kid yourself into thinking you won when you really lost. Why do people only talk about the isolated wins and forget the bottom line? Can you imagine running a business that way? Try telling your banker about the nice big order you got and how busy your office was, conveniently forgetting the most important part of the story: You never got paid. The customer went under. You lost. Tell your banker the truth, all of it, all the way to the bottom line. Tell your friends. Tell yourself.

THE COLOR OF MONEY

I remember the day my son came to me and wanted fifty bucks for a Nintendo game cartridge. That game computer I bought him for Christmas has ended up costing me an arm and a leg in game cartridges. We had just gotten back from our family vacation to Vegas and now Johnny wants a new video game to play. Incidentally, Vegas is no fun for kids, trust me. Disneyland is Disneyland. Las Vegas is Las Vegas, okay?

Anyhow, I told him what other parents tell their kids: "Fifty bucks is a lot of money."

"But Dad, it's only fifty dollars." (My son still thinks checks just automatically come in the mail, but things do change: Now it's fifty bucks to take his girlfriend out to dinner).

"Johnny, I'm not going to just give you fifty bucks. I work hard for my money. You'll play the game a few times and then lose it in a drawer somewhere."

"But Dad, I saw you lose $200 at that dice table, and you told Mom that it was nothing."

"Well, uh, yeah, but, uh…" (I told you Vegas is no place for kids!)

So he got the cartridge.

It is indeed unfortunate how we all put different labels on money, depending on where we are or what we're doing. I suppose it's too easy to say that all money is the same color; it goes in one ear and out the other. Every gambler has been a victim of this charade. I know it and you know it. For some reason, fifty dollars, a hundred dollars or even five hundred dollars diminishes in value when you're standing at a dice table. And I firmly believe that craps distorts these values more than any other casino game. Why? Because of the pace and the multitude of bets that are offered. The game is fast and the temptation to make more than just the low-percentage bets can be irresistible. A few rolls and all of a sudden you have more money in action than you realized.

It's a fact. Casino ratings of credit players who play both blackjack and craps typically show an average bet at the dice tables (all the bets in action at any given time, excluding odds) to be nearly three times as high as a single blackjack wager. So not only do the values diminish, the exposure increases at the same time. The casino is "psyching" you out of your money!

And then there's the matter of chips. The casinos don't use chips for convenience. They use chips to help blur the images of our valued friends Mr. Jackson, Mr. Grant, and Mr. Franklin. With plastic chips to play with, our concept of real money gets

a little fuzzy. But it all returns to sharp focus when we get home. I've always believed this is such an important aspect of gambling—recognizing and maintaining values—that I want to give you just one more example. And once again, the story comes from the racetrack:

My gambling buddy had just returned from Maywood (a harness track in Chicago), and told me he had won a couple hundred. He said it sounded pretty good at the time—until he "got back to the real world." What he meant, of course, is until he got home and saw his property tax bill for two grand, his doctor bills for five hundred, the insurance payment that was due (it's now double because his kid is driving), and finding out how much his daughter's tuition was going to be next year. Sure, we understand. At the track, the winnings were nice but a couple hundred isn't going to help much at home.

Time out!

Isn't that just another example of diminishing value? Did the $200 all of a sudden shrink to $100 as soon as he got home? I'll take a $200 win over a $200 loss every time. And I'll spend that $200 the same way I'd spend it if I had gone out and bused tables to earn it. We all tend to diminish the value of a gambling loss to help rationalize our worries—but here's a guy who diminishes the value of a gambling win. He's disappointed when he loses and disappointed when he wins!

I wonder if he'd be interested in one slightly used Nintendo. After all, a couple hundred bucks is nothing.

HOW TO FEEL GOOD
ABOUT YOURSELF

After a big loss, it's easy to say, "Boy, did I screw up! I nearly ruined my whole trip. I'm never going to do that again." But most of you will. Next week, next month, maybe even in the next hour. And when it does happen again, the real hurt is not going to be in your pocket but in your heart. You're going to feel bad about yourself, highly disappointed in yourself. I want to try to help you stop that from happening. Dealing with a financial loss is one thing. Dealing with a psychological loss is much worse. And wouldn't you know it? It's all in the timing.

Let's use smoking as an example. It's easy to want to quit when you don't want a cigarette, like the time when you polished off half a pack at the dice tables and then started coughing so badly. Remember? People looked at you like you were dying. You took one draw on that "last" cigarette and then snuffed it out in disgust: "I'm never going to buy any more of these things!" You remember, don't you, when your cigarette headache was so bad you got double vision? "Was that a hard 8? It was a 7? It looked like a hard 8 to me!" Yeah, quitting at that moment was too easy. But it's another story when you're on your third day of quitting and the guy next to you at the table is chain-smoking. Sniff, sniff: "Hey, blow it this way, will you buddy?" You know you're in trouble when everyone at the table looks like Joe Camel. Suffice to say, a dice table is a bad place to swear off smoking.

Oh, you don't smoke? Well then, plug in vodka martinis. Don't drink? Well, that only leaves sex as the other notable vice, and I really don't want to go into any hard-luck sex situations at this time. At least not at the dice tables. Whatever your vice, it's the guy who can quit for good, who can resist the urge for the rest of his life and knows it, who feels damn good about himself. It's a major accomplishment. The alcoholic who pushes aside one temptation after another feels very, very good about himself. If there's nothing about you to feel good about, if you continually disappoint yourself, life can be rough.

The next time you know that you shouldn't call your host for a room comp because it's going to cost you, so you don't make the call, you'll feel good about yourself. When you've got a few hundred in front of you and you're tired of playing anyhow, so you actually walk away from the table, you'll feel good about it. There's a tremendous amount of personal pride in walking away a winner. When you've acquired the discipline to actually walk around the casino with chips in your hand and resist playing them, you'll feel good that you have control over things. They don't have control over you. (This is a test I recommend everyone take)

Indeed there is another vice, the "G" word. If gambling doesn't work for you, maybe it's time to find something else to look forward to. The name of this game, my dear friend, is feeling good. About yourself. And if gambling doesn't make you feel good, then walk and keep walking. I don't want to encourage you to do anything that makes you feel bad inside.

> The road to self-respect begins when you stop doing the things you know you shouldn't do.

SUMMARY

Throughout this book, I've tried to give you a different kind of advice about gambling in general—the kind of advice that few other authors ever talk about. The most common of the gambling books simply teach you how to play the games, where to place your bet, and what payoffs to expect. It just isn't enough.

There's a huge difference between knowing how to play and knowing how to win. Casinos want you to know how to play the games and they'll even help you learn. But they won't help you win!

I like to see players who are aggressive—the *right* kind at the *right* time—and have a "sky's the limit" dream when they sense an opportunity. I want players to have confidence in their play, but not become overconfident. Equally important, I hope this book has impressed upon you the essential quality of maintaining discipline in your play. If you walk up to a nearly empty dice table and ask the stickman how it's going and he says, "Oh, boy, the dice are really cold," what are you going to do? What if it's the only table open and you badly want to play? Are you going to play? If you do, then I can only tell you I wish I owned my own casino and all my players were just like you— because that's what discipline isn't. If you accomplish anything by playing other than losing money, you only embarrassed yourself in front of the dice crew. "Hey, buddy. I told you the dice were cold!"

In this closing chapter, I've answered some tough personal questions. Now let me ask you one. When you first enter a casino, what thoughts are going through your head? Are they negative thoughts or positive thoughts? Do you feel conditioned to win? Or do you feel conditioned to lose? See if what I'm about to tell you rings any bells. Overheard in a casino: "We didn't win anything; we only lost a few hundred dollars; but we had fun!" Whoa! Don't ever let your gambling reach the point where losing is fun. Losing is not fun. Winning is fun!

There's something else I want to see in players, and that's a certain cynicism in their attitude about the odds and the percentages they're facing. Basically, I don't want to see players trusting those odds, because odds can be very misleading to the inexperienced. I've always believed that a casino is no place to be in a trusting mood.

Do you think you'll be able to develop a kind of intuition, an ability to listen to your inner self? That uncanny predictability we covered earlier is just as hard to define here as it was before. If you feel it in your heart, forget it; if you feel it in your guts, believe it—and then do it! The casino isn't a place for compassion; it's a jungle where only the tough survive through their cunning instinct. I also want to see a trait that is equally hard to find. A satisfaction, if you will, a state of being satisfied without reaching your dream limits. Learn how to be satisfied with any sort of win, because winning beats losing every time. And there's always a next time to try again. I consider this the number one trait of a tough player: Take what you can get!

All of this is not to say that being properly psyched up is enough either. You do have to pick up on all the aspects of any game you want to play. That's something every sharp player learns at the very outset. Some bets are better than others; some games sport different rules; some games are just not worth playing. You have to know all these things too.

Above all, I want you to play fairly. Show a little respect for the games, the dealers, and your fellow players, whether you win or lose. And you'll earn some respect for yourself. Good Luck!

TIPS FROM A 30-YEAR GAMBLER

1. If you think you're going to lose, you probably will. If you're anxious to win, you probably won't. Most players are conditioned to lose before they even enter a casino. Think positive!

2. Observe before you play. There's so much to be gained by just watching. If nothing else, you'll never plop yourself down at a cold table. Sure, we all know that tables turn, but wise gamblers know that tables tend to stay the course.

3. Play in sessions that are short and sweet. Take frequent breaks, quit when you're ahead, and quit when you're losing. Unless you're on an incredible win streak, never play in marathon sessions!

4. Always begin play with relatively small wagers. When you're winning, increase your bets, though sensibly. When you're losing, decrease your bets or quit the session. You can always go back later. This rule is the hallmark of top players.

5. Never set limits on your winnings. Let the sky be the limit. But do set strict limits on losses.

6. If you lose two bets in a row, change tables or take a break. I never lose three bets in a row at the same table. Never!

7. Let your intuitive senses take over as you size up a casino. Follow gut feelings. Forget superstitions. Leave your systems at home.

8. Get smarter. Study the games, especially the vulnerable games such as blackjack or poker.

9. Shop for the best games. There are differences! Video poker paytables, prop bet payoffs at the dice tables, and player-option rules at the blackjack tables are just some examples. Don't get suckered in to a sucker game.

10. Never show off. You're not playing to impress others. Big bets won't make you a better player. Big bets won't change the cards.

11. Be wary of comps. They are the casino's most effective marketing tool. Remember, the casino is never going to do anything for you that will help you win!

12. Think twice before you apply for credit in a casino. Easy come, easy go.

13. Never play if you are tired or moody or have too many things on your mind. You must have a clear head and feel up to the challenge. Don't start round 1 feeling like you just finished round 12.

14. You must learn how to be focused on your objective. Don't let other things interfere with your goal: To win!

15. Avoid speeding. If dealers are running a table game too fast for you, walk away. At the slot machines, there are no "fastest finger" awards. You control the speed. So slow it down and enjoy yourself.

16. Take only the bankroll that you know from past experiences is right for you. Too little might make you play far too conservatively. Too much might make you play with the wrong type of aggression. Bankroll should never be a source of confidence.

17. Budget your bankroll so that it will cover your trip. If you plan to gamble for three days, first divide your bankroll into thirds. If you plan five sessions per day, divide each third into fifths, one for each session.

18. You work hard for your money, right? Let go of it hard, too.

19. Never bet against a trend. Wise gamblers always bet with a streak, never against it.

20. Tip the dealers only if they are polite, helpful, and competent. Tip only at the end of a winning session. And be sensible about it.

21. Make your gambling a planned destination trip; never go gambling on a whim.

22. Play on weekdays. You'll have more choices and more space. Weekends, or whenever the casino is busy, is never a good time to play.

23. Don't believe everything your friends tell you. Casino games are rife with bad advice, especially in the case of slot machines. They are never overdue. They are never ready to hit. Payouts are determined by a computer chip inside each machine. Every spin produces a purely random event; completely unpredictable.

24. I have a habit of sharing some of my winnings with players who are less fortunate, especially those who are down on their luck. It may not be for you, but for me it has completely changed my take on winning and losing. Try it.

25. If you can't afford to lose it, don't bet it.

THE CARDOZA CRAPS MASTER
Exclusive Offer! - Not Available Anywhere Else)
Three Big Strategies!

Here It Is! **At last**, the **secrets** of the **Grande-Gold Power Sweep**, **Molliere's Monte Carlo Turnaround** and the **Montarde-D'Girard Double Reverse** - three big strategies - are made available and presented for the **first time anywhere**! These powerful strategies are designed for the serious craps player, one wishing to bring the best odds and strategies to hot tables, cold tables and choppy tables.

I. THE GRANDE-GOLD POWER SWEEP (HOT TABLE STRATEGY)

This **dynamic strategy** takes maximum advantage of hot tables and shows you how to amass small **fortunes quickly** when numbers are being thrown fast and furious. The Grande-Gold stresses aggressive betting on wagers the house has no edge on! This previously unreleased strategy will make you a powerhouse at a hot table.

2. MOLLIERE'S MONTE CARLO TURNAROUND (COLD TABLE STRATEGY)

For the player who likes betting against the dice, Molliere's Monte Carlo Turnaround shows how to turn a cold table into hot cash. Favored by an exclusive circle of professionals who will play nothing else, the uniqueness of this strongman strategy is that the vast majority of bets **give absolutely nothing away to the casino**!

3.MONTARDE-D'GIRARD DOUBLE REVERSE (CHOPPY TABLE STRATEGY)

This **new** strategy is the **latest development** and the **most exciting strategy** to be designed in recent years. **Learn how** to play the optimum strategies against the tables when the dice run hot and cold (a choppy table) with no apparent reason. **The Montarde-d'Girard Double Reverse** shows how you can **generate big profits** while less knowledgeable players are ground out by choppy dice. And, of course, the majority of our bets give nothing away to the casino!

BONUS!!! Order now, and you'll receive **The Craps Master-Professional Money Management Formula** ($15 value) **absolutely free**! Necessary for serious players and **used by the pros**, the Craps Master Formula features the unique **stop-loss ladder**.

The Above Offer is Not Available Anywhere Else. You Must Order Here.

To order send ~~$75~~ $50 (plus postage and handling) by check or money order to:
Cardoza Publishing, P.O. Box 98115, Las Vegas, NV 89193

WIN MONEY PLAYING CRAPS!
$25 Off! (with this coupon)

YES, I want to take advantage of this **exclusive** offer and learn these **newly revealed** strategies. Please **rush** me the **CSB Craps Master** and the **bonus**. Enclosed is a check or money order for $50 (plus postage and handling) made out to:
Cardoza Publishing, P.O. Box 98115, Las Vegas, NV 89193

MC/Visa/Amex Orders Toll-Free in U.S. & Canada, 1-800-577-WINS

Include $5.00 postage/handling for U.S. orders; $10.00 for Can/Mex; HI/AK and other countries $15.00. Outside U.S., money order payable in U.S. dollars on U.S. bank only.

NAME _____

ADDRESS _____

CITY _____ STATE _____ ZIP _____

MC/Visa/Amex Orders By Mail

MC/Visa/Amex # _____ Phone _____

Exp. Date _____ Signature _____

30 Day Money Back Guarantee!

What Casinos Don't

FREE!
Poker & Gaming Magazines

www.cardozabooks.com

3 GREAT REASONS TO VISIT NOW!

1. FREE GAMING MAGAZINES
Go online now and read all about the exciting world of poker, gambling, and online gaming. Our magazines are packed with tips, expert strategies, tournament schedules and results, gossip, news, contests, polls, exclusive discounts on hotels, travel, and more to our readers, prepublication book discounts, free-money bonuses for online sites, and words of wisdom from the world's top experts and authorities. Also, you can opt-in for Avery Cardoza's free email newsletters.

2. MORE THAN 200 BOOKS TO MAKE YOU A WINNER
We are the world's largest publisher of gaming and gambling books and represent a who's who of the greatest players and writers on poker, gambling, chess, back-gammon, and other games. With more than nine million books sold, we know what our customers want. Trust us.

3. THIS ONE IS A SURPRISE
Visit us now to get the goods!

So what are you waiting for?
CARDOZA PUBLISHING ONLINE

Gambler's Book Club
Las Vegas, Nevada

Shop online at the Gambler's Book Club in Las Vegas. Since 1964, the GBC has been the reigning authority on gambling publications and one of the most famous gaming institutions. We have the world's largest selection of gaming, gambling and casino management books—more than 3,000 titles in stock. Go online now!

702-382-7555
www.gamblersbookclub.com